Redesigning the Unremarkable

Redesigning the Unremarkable is a timely and necessary reminder that the often neglected elements and spaces of our built environment – from trash bins, seats, stairways, and fences to streets, bikeways, underpasses, parking lots, and shopping centres – must be thoughtfully redesigned to enhance human and planetary health. Using the lens of sustainable, salutogenic, and playable design, in this inspiring book, Miller and Cushing explore the challenges, opportunities, and importance of redesigning the unremarkable. Drawing on global research, theory, practical case studies, photographs, and personal experiences, *Redesigning the Unremarkable* is a vital text – a doer's guide – for researchers, policymakers, and practitioners wanting to transform and positively reimagine our urban environment.

Evonne Miller is Professor of Design Psychology and Director of the QUT Design Lab, at Queensland University of Technology in Brisbane, Australia. With research expertise in participatory co-design and design for health, her previous books include *Creating Great Places: Evidence-based Urban Design for Health and Wellbeing* (2020, with Cushing) and *Creative Arts-Based Research in Aged Care: Photovoice, Photography and Poetry in Action* (2021), both published by Routledge.

Debra Flanders Cushing is Associate Professor in Landscape Architecture in the School of Architecture and Built Environment at Queensland University of Technology. Her research combines her interest in healthy and supportive environments for young people and intergenerational populations, with her understanding of using design theory and research evidence to create sustainable and vibrant landscapes. She uses environmental psychology theory and placemaking principles to evaluate and understand the design of cities and outdoor spaces and is the author of *Creating Great Places: Evidence-based Urban Design for Health and Wellbeing* (2020, with Miller).

Redesigning the Unremarkable

Evonne Miller and
Debra Flanders Cushing

NEW YORK AND LONDON

Designed cover image: © Getty Images

First published 2023
by Routledge
605 Third Avenue, New York, NY 10158

and by Routledge
4 Park Square, Milton Park, Abingdon, Oxon, OX14 4RN

Routledge is an imprint of the Taylor & Francis Group, an informa business

© 2023 Evonne Miller and Debra Flanders Cushing

The right of Evonne Miller and Debra Flanders Cushing to be identified as authors of this work has been asserted in accordance with sections 77 and 78 of the Copyright, Designs and Patents Act 1988.

All rights reserved. No part of this book may be reprinted or reproduced or utilised in any form or by any electronic, mechanical, or other means, now known or hereafter invented, including photocopying and recording, or in any information storage or retrieval system, without permission in writing from the publishers.

Trademark notice: Product or corporate names may be trademarks or registered trademarks, and are used only for identification and explanation without intent to infringe.

ISBN: 978-0-367-51190-6 (hbk)
ISBN: 978-0-367-51189-0 (pbk)
ISBN: 978-1-003-05274-6 (ebk)

DOI: 10.4324/9781003052746

Typeset in Sabon
by KnowledgeWorks Global Ltd.

Contents

List of figures   vii
List of tables   ix

1 Why focus on the unremarkable?   1

Section I: Unremarkable elements   **27**

2 Throwing out: Redesigning trash bins and landfills to be more remarkable   29

3 Sitting down: Redesigning benches and chairs to be more remarkable   44

4 Moving up: Redesigning stairs to be more remarkable   62

5 Blocking out: Redesigning walls and fences to be more remarkable   78

Section II: Unremarkable spaces   **95**

6 Passing under: Redesigning underpasses to be more remarkable   97

7 Strolling along: Redesigning streets and sidewalks to be more remarkable   112

8 Going places: Redesigning bikeways and multi-use trails to be more remarkable   126

9 Staying put: Redesigning parking lots to be remarkable   141

vi Contents

10 Spending time and money: Redesigning shopping centres
to be remarkable 158

Conclusion: Redesigning the unremarkable – thinking
differently 177

Appendix 178
Acknowledgements 181
Index 182

Figures

1.1	Yarn-bombing in suburban Brisbane, Australia, and France	2
1.2	When urban elements and spaces are unremarkable: a fence, a bench, and a sidewalk	5
1.3	DIY urbanism – child-friendly street signs	11
1.4	Examples of sustainable spaces and elements	14
1.5	Examples of salutogenic elements and spaces	16
1.6	Examples of playable elements and spaces	18
1.7	Making a fence playable	20
2.1	A gumdrop bin, on an urban street	32
2.2	Public trash bin where graphic design uses humour to nudge sustainability	34
2.3	The world's first voting ashtray	38
2.4	CopenHill in Copenhagen, Denmark –site of waste, park, and ski slope	39
3.1	Benches in Harvard Plaza designed by Stoss Landscape Urbanism	49
3.2	A bench is poorly placed with its back to a busy road in downtown Brisbane	51
3.3	One of the benches from the Red Bench Project, located in Indooroopilly, Queensland, Australia	53
3.4	Melancholy by sculpture artist Albert Gyorgy	54
3.5	Swing Time at the Boston Convention Center	57
3.6	Colin Selig's sculptural benches made from recycled propane tanks	58
4.1	External stairs at Darling Harbor, Sydney, Australia	65
4.2	The Cascade Project in Hong Kong	67
4.3	The black and white spiral staircase of Oodi Helsinki Central Library	68
4.4	Stairs and elevator decals	73
5.1	Cheerful flower paintings cover up graffiti on an overpass embankment	81
5.2	Walls and fences that can contribute to place identity and sense of place	82
5.3	An example of a green wall in Denmark	84

viii **Figures**

5.4	Unique construction fencing that showcases Indigenous art on the Queensland University of Technology campus in Australia	87
5.5	Simple hearts are attached to a chain link fence to add colour and life to a plain fence near a parking lot	90
6.1	A lush urban plaza underneath railroad infrastructure, designed by RPS Group	102
6.2	Burnside Skatepark in Portland, Oregon	106
6.3	Water themed underpass in Rockhampton, Australia	107
6.4	The Rainbow Tunnel in Toronto	107
6.5	The Silly Walks Tunnel in the Netherlands	108
7.1	Connecting during COVID-19 – chalk hopscotch and teddy bears in trees	113
7.2	When streets and sidewalks are unremarkable in design	114
7.3	A streatery in street parking in Melbourne	117
8.1	Multi-use trail with separated bicycle and pedestrian lanes	130
8.2	Examples of pathways that end abruptly from Brisbane, Australia	131
8.3	An efficient, but poorly designed bikeway on the left compared to a well-designed multi-use trail on the right	134
8.4	The Hovenring roundabout in Eindhoven, the Netherlands	136
9.1	Example of a parking lot solar canopy, at Google corporate headquarters	147
9.2	Rooftop public space and harbour views at Parking House + Konditaget Lüders	152
9.3	Roof top playground, running track and exercise at Parking House + Konditaget Lüders	152
9.4	Exterior stairs and frieze of Parking House + Konditaget Lüders	153
10.1	Adaptive re-use and sustainable retail at Burwood Brickworks	164
10.2	A striking indigenous mural on the internal ceiling of Burwood Brickwork	166
10.3	The redesign of Funan Singapore, featuring an urban farm	168
10.4	The redesign of Funan Singapore, featuring an indoor climbing wall and red biking track	171

Tables

7.1	Inexpensive and easily deployable traffic calming and pedestrian-priority street design strategies	118
10.1	Five critical changes in shopping centres for the post-pandemic world	161
10.2	A vision for the future – provocative scenarios for sustainable retail design	169

1 Why focus on the unremarkable?

The city of Brisbane in Australia announced, in June 2019, plans to redevelop a large inner-city golf course into a new 45-hectare public park. In recognition of the layered historical and cultural context of the site, the park will be given the dual name of Victoria Park/ Barrambin – the original Indigenous name for the area. Modelled after places like Central Park in New York City, Lumpini Park in Bangkok, and Hyde Park in London, this new multi-functional park (in our home city) will offer trees, playgrounds, and a public greenspace for community relaxation, interactions, and connections. As populations expand in urban areas, investment in such large-scale public space initiatives is critical and contributes significantly to the sustainability, liveability, playability, and simple beauty of our environments. What is significant about this redevelopment is that unless they live near it, most people will visit such high-profile public spaces infrequently – at the most, every month or so. In fact, we spend most of our time within local settings, located within a relatively small radius from our homes, our schools, and our workplaces. Our experience of those local urban environments, and their neglected micro-features, has a powerful impact on our health and well-being – yet these local spaces in which we conduct our daily lives are too often bland, boring, and, quite simply, unremarkable.

Why the unremarkable is important

Redesigning the Unremarkable argues for a different approach to urban redevelopment. Alongside the large-scale, high-profile urban development initiatives designed to positively transform cities (think, e.g., The High Line Park in New York City, Atlanta's BeltLine, the Cheonggyecheon Stream Restoration Project in Seoul, and Bilbao's transformation from industrial centre into a city of culture in Spain), we propose that we lower our gaze to look at and think – on a smaller scale – about the everyday, often neglected elements and spaces of our local urban environments.

Great design is not just important for the flagship architectural and master-planned projects. It is also the invisible, ordinary, and often

DOI: 10.4324/9781003052746-1

neglected elements and infrastructure – the streets, the sidewalks and alleys, the multi-use trails, the seating, the trash and recycling bin areas, as well as the bus stops, the parking lots, the highway and bridge underpasses, stairwells, and local shopping centres. It is these often mundane features of our everyday urban environments that still have a strong impact on how a place is experienced and perceived. It is these urban components that are far too often *unremarkable* in their design and appearance – yet have unlimited potential to contribute to vibrant urban life that fosters healthy living, social connections, joy, and happiness. Paying attention to these ordinary spaces and ensuring that these smaller urban elements – which are often forgotten, left-over, or not actually designed – is crucial, as they are what we engage with on a human scale and help define how a place is seen, touched, and experienced.

Promisingly, it often takes relatively little effort to transform the bland, boring, or broken aspects of our local urban environments. Simple, thoughtful, and creative changes – whether they are government- or citizen-led – can transform an unremarkable experience into something remarkable. Consider, for instance, the yarn-bombing depicted in Figure 1.1. My daily walk to the train station is made more enjoyable thanks to craft activists, who placed a knitted cover over a fire hydrant and in trees in a suburban street near where I live. This example of small-scale 'do-it-yourself' urbanism can have a positive impact on daily life. Even the addition of a patchwork blanket to a bench in Sèvres France (Figure 1.1) injects a wonderful sense of place, warmth, and joy to what was previously a bland environment. Adding vibrant colour and something unexpected to an otherwise ordinary scene can potentially make a significant difference in how we experience and relate to our environments – which in turn helps to foster health and happiness. See Chapter 5 for more on yarn-bombing.

Figure 1.1 Yarn-bombing in suburban Brisbane, Australia, and France.
Credit: Evonne Miller and So_P (Flickr, CC).

Similar examples across the globe show how creative thinking and inspired design have combined to enhance our public realm – and it is these smaller-scale everyday spaces, and the artefacts within these spaces, on which this book focuses. *Redesigning the Unremarkable* explores how both design professionals and inhabitants of cities are actively reshaping their public realm – and creating great places to live that are not only functional but also inspirational and forward-thinking. From creative 'yarn-bombed' streets to musical staircases, the creative details of a city come in multiple scales and can incorporate a variety of activities and elements.

We have written this book to challenge the way in which ordinary and everyday places and elements are created, often without much thought to how people interact with their environment and how those spaces might impact health and well-being – both positively and negatively. Too often, the spaces and elements that are the focus of this book are not purposefully or thoughtfully designed but haphazardly created. Sometimes they are expertly engineered to function safely, but without significant attention to aesthetics or how thoughtful design contributes to the experience of a unique place. This is important, as our experience of everyday places significantly impacts how we think, feel, and act.

In this book, we provide a critical examination of the unremarkable, providing thought-provoking and speculative examples of how they can be improved. Other authors have outlined the theoretical and practical discourses guiding urban planning and design, discussed the challenge of implementing global initiatives (such as the United Nations New Urban Agenda and Sustainable Development Goals), and reflected on how technological innovation and the emergence of 'the smart city' are transforming design practice (see, e.g., Brown & Dixon, 2014; Egenhoefer, 2018; Müller & Shimizu, 2018; Wheeler, 2013). As a complement to these efforts, we provide an examination of the mundane, micro-details of the urban environment – the focus of this book, which encourages designers, urban planners, and citizens to look critically and creatively at how local environments might be improved.

From broken to beautiful – why place aesthetics matter

In understanding the importance of the unremarkable, and how the environment influences people, we build on the seminal work of Kurt Lewin's (1936) behaviour equation: $B = f(P,E)$. Lewin argues that an individual's behaviour (B) is a function (f) of the Person (P), and their Environment (E), and to change behaviours, we must change the person or the environment. In *Redesigning the Unremarkable*, our focus is on how we might purposely change specific and often neglected elements

4   **Why focus on the unremarkable?**

of our urban environment, to foster sustainability, health and well-being, and play. As we focus specifically on the importance of design to support the experience of place, three key theoretical and conceptual frameworks provide a solid rationale: *broken window theory*; *cues to care*; and *nudge theory*.

Broken Window Theory, first introduced by Wilson and Kelling (1982), and further explored by Kelling and Coles (1996), suggests that minor visual elements of disorder such as litter, graffiti, or a broken window can communicate a disregard for maintenance, an invitation for crime and anti-social behaviour, or actually lead to crime. The premise is that a broken window signals a lack of social control, neighbourhood decay, and disorganisation. In an article written for *The Atlantic Monthly*, Wilson and Kelling (1982) reflected on the impact of a programme that assigned police officers 'walking beats' in New Jersey neighbourhoods. While the programme did not reduce crime rates, the visible presence of police on the streets meant residents felt safer, and minor disturbances and physical signs of social disorder (e.g. graffiti, litter, or broken windows) were immediately addressed. And although police patrolling an area is not technically a physical design intervention, it signals the potential impact of environmental cues.

The neglected urban spaces and elements can be perceived as a lack of care by the local government and community members, as well as the presence of incivilities and crime that are out of control or unmanaged. Although these elements may not directly relate to crime rates in a given urban area, they likely impact neighbourhood satisfaction and pride of place (Hur & Nasar, 2014). Research shows that the perceived physical upkeep of a neighbourhood positively impacts whether residents are satisfied with their neighbourhood. Both *temporary* signs of disorder, such as litter, and *semi-permanent* signs, such as broken windows or a property with a chain-link fence, can significantly impact the level of neighbourhood satisfaction (Hur & Nasar, 2014). For example, when people see litter specifically, they are more likely to anticipate physical incivilities (e.g. graffiti, vandalism, and vacant or dilapidated buildings) and social incivilities (e.g. anti-social behaviour, begging, gangs, and alcohol abuse; Medway et al., 2016). And in places with a lot of litter, people perceive an increase in crime.

The core argument is simple: visual cues of physical and social disorder in public spaces send a clear message that no one cares for this place, as we see in Figure 1.2. Fixing these problems when they are small (i.e. quickly repairing a broken window) means smaller problems are less likely to escalate into big problems, signalling to the broader community that this place is actively monitored and cared for (Kelling & Coles, 1996; Wilson & Kelling, 1982). Fixing broken windows immediately improves the quality of urban life. If the physical

Why focus on the unremarkable? 5

Figure 1.2 When urban elements and spaces are unremarkable: a fence, a bench, and a sidewalk.

Credit: Michael Coghlin (Flickr CC); Debra Cushing; Evonne Miller.

environment feels safe, then people are more likely to use it, which in turn improves the safety and vitality of the space, as people provide informal surveillance.

This concept of broken windows is reminiscent of Jane Jacobs' classic *'eyes on the street'* argument. In *The Death and Life of Great American Cities*, Jacobs (1961) astutely argues that a vibrant street life is critical to neighbourhood safety and a connected community. She emphatically stated that citizen vigilance was more important than the police, as public peace was 'kept primarily by an intricate, almost unconscious network of voluntary controls and standards among the people themselves, and enforced by the people themselves' (1961, p. 41). Maximising informal surveillance, also referred to as natural surveillance in the Crime Prevention through Environmental Design (CPTED) literature, and the presence of friendly 'eyes on the street' however, requires an attractive built environment context that offers legitimate opportunities for people to spend time in one place, their local place.

Taking 'cues to care' into the urban realm

From our perspective, therefore, *Broken Window Theory* outlines why caring about the unremarkable is critical. Yet, we can't stop there. Signalling care and promoting positive action is the basis of the 'cues to care' concept. Landscape architects may be familiar with the notion of 'cues to care', introduced by American landscape architect Joan Nassauer to describe symbols of maintenance and care within the context of ecological landscape restoration. Nassauer (1995) explained that 'landscape language that communicates human intention' provides a 'powerful vocabulary' that educates people about ecological function (p. 161). These cues that Nassauer referred to include cultural symbols that express acts of restoration or protection for otherwise 'messy' natural landscapes. A simple and very explicit example is a fence along a hiking trail with a sign stating that the area is closed for rehabilitation by the local park service organisation. The fence and sign are recognised cultural symbols that communicate a specific message. They are cues to care.

Redesigning the Unremarkable takes the language of 'cues to care' into the urban design realm. When applied in conjunction with *Broken Window Theory*, we can incorporate simple cultural symbols and creative design interventions to communicate that a neighbourhood is being watched over and cared for, rather than a hotspot for crime. You may have noticed Neighbourhood Watch signs posted on residential streets or in open spaces. These formal signs indicate the community is connected, and people are looking out for each other. Going beyond signage to focus on the design of the elements and spaces of the environment can also 'nudge' people to behave in certain ways – the basis of the nudge theory and the third theory to underpin our premise.

How thoughtful design nudges healthy behaviours

As planners, landscape architects, urban designers, and policymakers work to create urban environments that are friendly, safe, and active, there is increasing interest in interventions that 'nudge' residents towards positive behaviours and interactions. Richard Thaler (awarded the 2017 Nobel Memorial Prize in Economic Sciences) introduced the term and concept of a 'nudge' into the lexicon with his 2008 book *Nudge: Improving Decisions about Health, Wealth and Happiness*, co-authored with Cass Sunstein. In the book, they define a nudge as 'any aspect of the choice architecture that alters people's behaviour in a predictable way without forbidding any options or significantly changing their economic incentives' (p. 6).

Thaler and Sunstein (2008) describe their behavioural economics approach as libertarian paternalism, in that nudge theory recognises that people must still have the ability to choose (libertarian) but also attempts to 'steer people's choices in directions that will improve their lives' (paternalism) (p. 5). The subtle change of placing water, fruit, and vegetables (not junk food) at eye level in cafeterias (the nudge) is a great example of how nudges can foster healthy eating. By designing the physical space so the healthy option is more prominent, seen first, and more enticing, we can begin to influence food choices. This concept can be applied to many different choices that people make daily.

Design is never neutral

Thaler and Sunstein remind us there is *'no such thing as a "neutral" design'* (p. 3). Even seemingly simple or arbitrary design decisions have significant impacts on people's behaviour. Consider, for example, the location and access to the stairwell in many office buildings. Like many people worried about the lack of physical movement in their daily lives, I recently decided to take the stairs (rather than the elevator) anytime I go up or down three stories or less. Recently, I was in the lobby of an unfamiliar government building and was unable to locate the stairs easily. All the nearby doors were unmarked, and the one I tried seemed to be locked. Essentially, the design of that lobby (and the decisions of the building managers) nudged me towards an *unhealthy* choice of taking the elevator and prevented me from being active.

When considered in conjunction with energy consumption, a single elevator trip could also be seen as the less sustainable option. In a situation like this, the stairwell is often behind a closed, non-descript metal door because of fire safety. Yet, a simple sign directing people to the stairs could have remedied this unfortunate design flaw in the short-term; the addition of a fire-safe glass door or internal window to make the stairwell visible, or the use of bright paint on the door or markings on the floor to provide wayfinding cues could be more permanent solutions. You can read more about nudging stair use in Chapter 4.

We can contrast this recent experience to the growing number of innovative initiatives across the globe that actively support incidental stair use by applying gamification and motivational messaging. Take, for example, the *Piano Stars*. As part of their Fun Theory campaign (based on the premise that we can change people's habits if we make it fun), car-manufacturer Volkswagen converted a set of stairs at the Odenplan subway station in Stockholm in 2009 into working piano keys. Instead of riding the escalator, commuters climbed the stairs, making music. This *nudge* resulted in an increased stair use of 66%! Although this short-term, one-day installation was estimated to cost AUD$50,000 (Crawley, 2010), with no evaluation or impact study published, anecdotally it made a big impact on healthy living. And it hopefully led to a few unexpected smiles during the dreaded morning commute! Many companies or organisations take this playful approach to incidental exercise further into the programming realm. The British Heart Foundation attempted to increase employee physical activity levels and overall well-being by challenging people to climb as many flights as possible as an individual or team competition, as we will see later in Chapter 4.

In addition to fostering fun and incidental exercise, the purposeful redesign of the built environment can also nudge pro-environmental behaviours. Take littering, for example. Again, as part of the Fun Theory campaign, Volkswagen developed the bottomless bin (when trash is dropped in, it triggers the sound effect of a long fall) and created a bottle bank arcade, which gives points to users for putting bottles in the right holes. Throwing rubbish away has also become a fun game in the Swiss city of Lucerne, where painted decals of games, such as mazes, hopscotch, and basketball, surround rubbish bins. And playful nudges even work in the most unusual circumstances, including men's urinals. Frustrated with men's seeming inability to aim, authorities at Schiphol Airport in Amsterdam etched 'an image of a black housefly into each urinal', a simple creative nudge that reduced spillage by 80% (Thaler & Sunstein, 2008).

As beautiful, intriguing, and inspiring as these creative nudges are, they remain the exception – not the rule – in our built environment. Consider an area you are familiar with, perhaps near your home or workplace. How many features in that local urban environment purposely – and creatively – foster health, well-being, happiness, or environmental sustainability? Most areas can be significantly improved, often through relatively little financial expense. And these small nudges can have a significant and positive impact on your quality of life.

The dark side of nudging: sludges and the paternalistic neo-liberal agenda

It would be remiss of us not to acknowledge the dark sides of nudges and nudging, which has been criticised for its potentially paternalistic utility and neo-liberal agenda. Dark nudges are nudges 'for bad', such as 'sludges' which make behaviour change difficult, rather than easy (e.g. adding details and processes that prevent people from getting a rebate or benefit, or easily opting out of a gym contract!).

Responding to ethical concerns about the rationale for and transparency of nudges for behaviour change, Hansen and Jespersen (2013) developed a typological framework outlining four types of nudges depending on the degree to which they were transparent or non-transparent, and the associated human judgement and cognitive thinking/decision-making processes, which are either reflexive or automatic. In transparent nudges, citizens easily see the intention – such as the painted footsteps leading towards a trash bin used by Keep Britain Tidy[1] designed to visually nudge people towards responsible litter disposal. In non-transparent nudges, intentions are hidden – for example, reducing plate sizes in a cafeteria (without telling people) which results in serving and eating less food. How we cognitively respond to such nudges varies, from automatic (fast, intuitive, and instinctive thinking, also known as System 1) to reflexive thinking (slow and deliberate, also known as System 2). As nudges purposely target cognitive, social, and behavioural biases and norms to influence decision-making and change behaviours, we must always reflect on the nature of and potential adverse impact of any policy or design nudge.

Place-making and the value of broken window, cues to care, and nudge theories

In many ways, the premise of broken windows, cues to care, and nudge theories implicitly underpin much contemporary place-making thought. Let's consider the emphasis on friendly, compact, and walkable neighbourhood design that is promoted through the New Urbanism movement. Human-scale design where housing, shopping, schools, parks and other public spaces are in close proximity to foster social and environmental sustainability. Streets are lined with shade trees and bordered by wide sidewalks to encourage walking, houses have front porches instead of stockade fencing to enable neighbourly interactions, parks include playgrounds and seating areas for socialising and playing, and shops include interesting and unique storefronts that are enticing. These large and small details are important and can make a big difference to how well a place functions and how people function within it. This movement essentially supports sustainable, playable, and salutogenic environments.

The emergence of the 'do it yourself' city

Although design professionals and community decision-makers often have a responsibility to initiate these small interventions within the urban environment, local residents too can take control and make small but impactful changes. For example, the yarn-bombing depicted in Figure 1.1, also known as guerrilla knitting, is a type of 'bottom-up', 'tactical', 'guerilla', 'pop-up', or DIY (do it yourself) urbanism where local residents take it upon themselves to address urban issues and improve their local spaces. Our earlier discussion of Broken Window Theory listed chain-link fencing in a residential neighbourhood as a feature that can often send a negative message. This fencing style can often look shabby and is used as a cheap fix to keep people out of a certain area, for either safety or security reasons, and often within industrial zones. Used in a residential area, it can look out of place and low-quality. But through DIY efforts, a chain-link fence can be transformed into something more remarkable.

Using what Iveson (2013, p. 941) calls 'micro-spatial urban practices', passionate individuals and groups are positively transforming their local communities through the installation of their own low-cost and usually unauthorised urban design interventions. In addition to yarn-bombing, there is also guerrilla gardening, in which civic-minded local residents plant fruits, vegetables, and flowers in public spaces; chair-bombing, which places homemade seating in public spaces (including the placement of self-built benches at bus stops); and street libraries, where weather-proof book shelves protect and promote the use of free books by people who live in the vicinity or are just passing by (Douglas, 2018; Finn, 2014). Again, we refer to Jane Jacob's powerful insights, 'cities have the capability of providing something for every-body, only because, and only when, they are created by everybody' (1961, p. 238). For example, as Figure 1.3 illustrates, citizens in sub-urban Brisbane have taken it upon themselves to add a home-made sign to the street notifying everyone that 'children play here'.

The practice of DIY urbanism has evolved over time and in some cases has been accepted and promoted within cities as public officials have become aware of the positive impact small changes can have. Graffiti was once seen as a calling card for gang activity (referred to as tagging), or an expression of hip hop culture, and often had negative connotations. In some instances, this is changing. The city of Glasgow, Scotland, for example, has embraced its graffiti as elaborate works of street art that help make the city special. Many are now commissioned, and in cities like Melbourne, New York City, and London, street art has become a tourist attraction, adding a vibrant yet gritty appeal to an area. You can now book a guided walking tour in these cities to see and learn about the street art – combining physical activity, a cultural experience, and an income source for the tour guide.

At other times, however, there is a conflict between DIY urbanists and local policymakers. Urban Food Street (UFS), located in Buderim, on Australia's Sunshine Coast is one such example. Starting in 2009 with one residents' desire for a lime tree, the UFS initiative expanded to 11 streets by 2015, producing locally grown vegetables, fruits, and herbs (including 300 cabbages and 900 kg of bananas) for more than 200 people. Most of the neighbours were involved in planting, weeding,

Why focus on the unremarkable? 11

Figure 1.3 DIY urbanism – child-friendly street signs.
Credit: Tobias Volbert.

watering, or jam-making. Yet, in 2017, the local council culled 18 of the fruit trees in front of one property – because the property owner did not obtain the required permits or public liability insurance (Halliday, 2018). This conflict highlights how, at times, residents and policymakers have different visions and priorities, varying according to the cultural, political, socio-economic, and environmental characteristics of a particular place. This example powerfully illustrates, as Fran Tonkiss (2014) reminds us in *Cities by Design: The Social Life of Urban Form*, that city-making is a social process: it is often the interplay (positive and negative) of formal and informal practices that intertwines to shape residents experience of urban environments.

Redesigning the unremarkable to be sustainable, salutogenic, and playable

Our premise in this book is that when unremarkable elements and spaces within the urban environment are better designed, important messages are sent about whether it is designed for them, is cared for (*Cues to Care* and *Broken Window Theory*), and how they can use the space to positively contribute to their health and well-being (*Nudge Theory*). Sometimes these urban cues should be obvious, to ensure the message is received loud and clear. Clear signage is one way to do this, but it should not become the default solution. Or perhaps it can be used to creatively educate, rather than directly instruct. At other times, subtle design interventions are more appropriate and can have a cumulative effect on daily experiences.

In our first book, *Creating Great Places*, we discussed how theory-storming and engaging with design theory enables the creation of great places where people thrive. We argued that design must purposely engage with and address key global priorities, including sustainable, child and age-friendly universal design. We apply a similar lens here, arguing that we must redesign the unremarkable elements and spaces of the urban environment in three key ways: *to be sustainable, to be salutogenic, and to be playable*.

Sustainable design – redesigning the unremarkable to be sustainable

Our first design priority in redesigning the unremarkable is to make these elements and spaces sustainable. Across the globe, there is an urgent realisation that tackling climate change will require radical, disruptive interventions, and thoughtful design can be a powerful force for positive action on climate change. Drawing on concepts of restorative and regenerative sustainability, biomimicry, living systems-thinking, cradle-to-cradle, and circular design, in the remainder of this book, we outline how unremarkable features might be redesigned to contribute to more sustainable urban living. The uncomfortable reality is that we are currently living through a new geologic time period, the Anthropocene: human-induced global ecological change, which is posing a catastrophic threat to humanity. As public health advocate Trevor Hancock et al. (2016) explain, humanity is on an ecologically unsustainable course:

> We have become a force that rivals nature: our activities are causing the climate to change, the Earth to heat up and the oceans to acidify; our pollutants are spread throughout the world and contaminate food chains almost everywhere; we are degrading and depleting key

resources such as forests, fisheries, corals, grasslands and topsoils that are central to the well-being and survival of humans and many other species.

(p. 245)

To survive, we must radically change how we live: to not only reduce our current impact, but also regenerate past impacts to create healthy, equitable, and sustainable futures (Hancock et al., 2016). A wealth of literature – from diverse disciplines including psychology, sociology, economics, education, and philosophy – documents why people distance themselves from the climate crisis and the challenge of motivating environmentally responsible behaviours. From a built environment and design perspective, our role is to foster the transition from sustainable to regenerative, environmentally enhancing, biophilic, and restorative cities connected with natural systems (Beatley, 2016; Newman et al., 2014; Roggema, 2022; Thomson & Newman, 2018). Transitioning to this alternative future, Zhou (2021) reminds us, will not be easy: we must be mindful of structural barriers, the norms and values underpinning dominant discourse, and the systems, products, places, and processes that discourage, encourage, and model resource-efficient practices.

In *Redesigning the Unremarkable*, our focus is on how we might creatively and thoughtfully redesign elements and spaces of the urban environment so that they support and nudge sustainability and pro-environmental behaviours. Many of our day-to-day activities of living, from material choices, to rubbish disposal practices, to transport choices, impact the environment. People's patterns of purchasing, consuming, and disposing tend to be quick and automatic (System 1 thinking mode), rather than slower and deliberately controlled (System 2 thinking mode); thus, to prompt reflection and disrupt daily habits, environmental researchers will often use information, social norms, design, and physical environmental cues.

For example, rates of recycling in Edinburgh, Scotland, increased 85% through a design nudge: residents were provided with a smaller size trash bin (140 litres) and a larger recycling bin (240 litres; Newsroom, 2015). In this book, we discuss how implicit and explicit design decisions impact the sustainability of our planet – and can be a means to nudge pro-environmental actions and impacts. While much has been written about large-scale sustainability initiatives in our built environment, such as green buildings and green walls, Figure 1.4 shows the value of smaller-scale changes: a bioswale (vegetation that collects and filters stormwater, see Chapter 9), a simple nudge to take the stairs instead of the elevator, and sustainable trash bins, one that is smart solar-compacting and one that where the signage reminds users that their trash goes straight to landfill!

14 Why focus on the unremarkable?

Figure 1.4 Examples of sustainable spaces and elements.
Credit: Debra Cushing; woodleywonderworks (Flickr CC 2.0); Evonne Miller; Debra Cushing.

Salutogenic design – redesigning the unremarkable to be salutogenic

Our second design priority in redesigning the unremarkable is how these elements and spaces might be designed to foster health and wellbeing, creating salutogenic cities. Salutogenic design is about creating health-promoting environments that are preventative, rather than reactive. It incorporates place-making principles to enable people to enjoy and be invigorated by the places in which they spend their time – enabling healthy, active living and quality of life.

This book was written as we experienced the COVID-19 global pandemic. With significant impacts felt throughout the world, this pandemic changed how most of us lived, worked, and played within our local environments. Many cities experienced lockdowns for significant periods of time which often severely limited the use of public space. Once lockdowns ended, social distancing was enforced and it limited the social engagement and connections that we were able to experience. Although the restrictions may be lifting, it offers us a powerful reminder that our environments are important and that focusing on our health and well-being is critical.

In addition, some of the social issues we refer to in this book, such as homelessness in Chapter 6, are complex systemic global issues. Although we believe in the power of place and that making small improvements can have major impacts, we are by no means suggesting that a simple mural or yarn-wrapped fence is enough to address these challenges. We understand that these societal challenges require complex long-term policies and programmes to effect sustainable and effective improvements. However, we also advocate for including changes to the physical environment as important components of any strategy. Positive changes to the built environment cannot be seen as tokenistic attempts to address challenges, but instead should be seen as key contributors to potential solutions.

Using place-making techniques to create vibrant places, as well as adding design nudges that enable people to be more physically active, socially engaged, and feeling calm within everyday spaces is important. We discuss how a proactive approach to create healthy urban environments often comes down to the details that can determine our daily actions, and help nudge people towards actions that are good for their mental, physical, and social well-being. Figure 1.5 shows some urban salutogenic spaces in Australia: an inviting boardwalk in a botanic garden, visually attractive stairs set among greenery on Australia's Gold Coast, an underpass in inner-urban Brisbane city featuring outdoor exercise equipment, a river-side multi-use trail, as well as spaces for family scooting in suburban Brisbane.

Playable design – redesigning the unremarkable to be playable

Finally, we turn our attention to the importance of play – the value of intentionally rethinking the design of unremarkable elements and spaces of our urban environment to be playable. Long recognised as the 'work' of children, play is an important objective for the design of playgrounds, parks, school grounds, and other spaces set aside for young people. As a mechanism to engage with and learn about the immediate environment, playfulness can also be an important aim for

16   Why focus on the unremarkable?

Figure 1.5 Examples of salutogenic elements and spaces.
Credit: Debra Cushing; Evonne Miller; Debra Cushing; Debra Cushing; Evonne Miller.

healthy and vibrant urban spaces – and was identified as a key principle in French theorist Henri Lefebvre's seminal book, *The Right to the City* (1968).

While we often link play to childhood, adults also regularly embrace play in different formats – sporting competitions, trivia challenges, and television game shows to name a few; yet much of our daily life activities are experienced as dull and mundane, and not at all playful. Playable design argues that purposefully creating opportunities for urban play – as well as offering a site for fun, joy, and pleasure – might also facilitate social interactions and connections, and thus tackle a major contemporary challenge: loneliness and social isolation. While loneliness is subjective, defined as the *feeling* of being alone, social isolation is having few social contacts to interact with.

Seen as a major global issue that affects many people, the United Kingdom has become the first country in the world to appoint a Minister for Loneliness, and statistics from the Harvard Graduate School of Education suggest a third (36%) of all Americans – and 61% of young adults and 51% of mothers with young children – feel 'serious loneliness', defined as feeling lonely 'frequently' or 'almost all the time or all the time' in the prior four weeks (Weissbourd et al., 2021). While this data was collected during the global coronavirus pandemic, it is commonly estimated one in three people feel lonely, which has negative health impacts (Holt-Lunstad et al., 2015). Redesigning our cities to facilitate connection and designing spaces, where all generations can interact through play, is one strategy for tackling loneliness. Playful urban spaces and elements that encourage children *and* adults to smile, laugh, challenge themselves, connect with others, be physically active, and simply enjoy life should not be limited to theme parks and sports arenas. We should be incorporating it into the unremarkable spaces of our daily activities. Figure 1.6 shows several examples of ways to make a space more playable including: projecting images on a pathway, installing ping pong tables in an underpass park, placing a koala sculpture on a bench in a botanic garden in Australia, using swinging seats in Boston, using thought-provoking signs, and creating playful benches from recycled propane tanks.

This is in fact the premise of the playable city movement, which uses typically mundane urban infrastructure and the affordances of smart technologies to create interactive, exciting, and memorable experiences (Nijholt, 2017; 2020). From public pianos as street furniture and large interactive displays on buildings and bus stops, the playable cities concept is challenging policymakers and residents to re-envision the design and use of public spaces to create playful and humorous interactions. The playable city movement, which originated in Bristol in the United Kingdom in 2012, positions people and play as

18 Why focus on the unremarkable?

Figure 1.6 Examples of playable elements and spaces.

Credit: Evonne Miller; Evonne Miller; Debra Cushing; John Horner; Courtesy of Höweler + Yoon Architecture; Evonne Miller; Colin Selig.

the heart of the future city, typically using smart city technologies to make urban infrastructure fun. Take, for example, *Stop Smile Stroll* – the winner of the 2016 Playable City Award.[2] This playful intervention temporarily turned the pedestrian crossing stop/walk lights into a shared moment of connection, inviting passers-by to show and share how they're feeling, using video, music, and augmented reality to reveal the collective 'mood of the moment'.

Of course, many have critiqued the focus on play, arguing that these 'cutesy distractions ... don't democratize cities' (np, O'Sullivan, 2016), don't offer real value (such as arrival time of the next bus or directions to the nearest hospital), are typically temporary installations only, and are seldom co-created in collaboration with diverse, real end users – children, older people, and people with disabilities (Nijholt, 2018). However, done well, the concepts of playable design and playable cities maximise the existing affordances of smart technologies (sensors, data processors, screens) with the smartness of city dwellers to make life more enjoyable. Purposefully introducing play, playfulness, and play-ability into urban settings supports placemaking, as Nijholt (2020) explains:

> Why introduce play into a city? Play can be considered one of the basic needs of human beings .... Rather than being involved in physical play ourselves, we can enjoy the playing of others, share the enjoyment with others, and experience a playful atmosphere in a city. We can sense a city and can develop affective feelings for a city because we experience it as being playful for us, for our chil-dren, for our friends, or for the community we live in.
>
> (p. 4)

In fact, as we will see, playable design can support health and well-being, through facilitating connections, conversations, and physical activity, with research also suggesting play and gamification could foster sustainability (Froehlich, 2015). Rivera et al. (2020) argue that we need to design and build *sustainable playable* cities, which enable and encourage mobility at a slow place, and enable and encourage play in all space – so that a playable city becomes a sustainable city. One such example is when the digital game Pokemon GO aligns with sustainability goals: you cannot score if you move too fast (travel by car, rather than walking) and you progress in the game if you play with people in your neighbourhood.

In this book, we discuss how a playful city can accommodate our innate need to explore, discover, experiment, and even test our mental and physical boundaries, while promoting our health, well-being and potentially, also the sustainability of our planet. Figure 1.7, for example, shows a fence in Brisbane that has been purposely designed for play.

Organisation of this book

We have divided this book into two sections – the first describes different, yet common, elements within urban environments, those often overlooked in terms of their potential contribution to the overall

Why focus on the unremarkable?

Figure 1.7 Making a fence playable.
Credit: Michael Langdon.

quality and impact of a space. Designing these elements is often an afterthought. The smaller elements, such as trash bins and benches, are usually chosen from a supplier catalogue and installed. Other elements, such as large retaining walls, are more carefully engineered and considered, but still may lack an awareness of their potential aesthetic contribution and how they might impact and positively contribute to the experience a space.

We have organised the elements according to the different actions they accommodate and have given each type of action its own chapter in order to dig deeper into its importance and contribution to a holistic urban design approach. Additionally, this book is best viewed as a source of inspiration and ideas for change; we will not be providing specific architectural, engineering, or industrial design specifications for the elements presented, but instead we explore conceptually what they might look like if they were redesigned with principles of sustainability, salutogenesis, or playable design at the forefront. Our intent is to challenge and extend current practice by raising awareness of what is and what might be – and while we have focused on these three key domains for change, we encourage readers to think more broadly and ask related questions about each element and space, such as *what would an sustainable street look like?*

Part 1: Four elements

1) **Throwing Out:** trash bins and landfills.
2) **Sitting Down:** benches and chairs.
3) **Moving Up:** stairways.
4) **Blocking Out:** walls and fences.

At this juncture, we acknowledge that the elements and spaces we discuss sit within a broader cultural and historical context. While a focus on Indigenous heritage and design is beyond the scope of this book, many of the examples, images, and stories shared here are from unique local contexts, with rich layered histories. There are a handful of projects that we mention that acknowledge and celebrate these histories, for example, the Bentway in Toronto which recognises the traditional territory of many nations on which the project occurs (Chapter 6) and in the Australian context; the purposeful use of local Aboriginal and Torres Strait Islander words to help with wayfinding and site identity for a new park (Chapter 1); and the use of Aboriginal and Torres Strait Islander images and stories on murals in shopping centres and on construction fencing (Chapters 5 and 10).

The second section of the book describes spaces, again, quite common and found in most cities in developed countries across the globe. Yet, they can be the spaces that are mundane, dirty, and even dangerous. These spaces are often created without a thorough understanding of their importance or potential to contribute to our health and well-being. Indeed, 15 years ago now, Australian landscape architect Elizabeth Mossop (2006) argued ubiquitous under-utilised infrastructural spaces (such as parking lots) should be designed and used much more strategically, noting that a:

> re-examination of infrastructural spaces involves the recognition that all types of space are valuable, not just the privileged spaces of more traditional parks and squares, and they must therefore

be inhabitable in a meaningful way. This requires the rethinking of the monofunctional realm of infrastructure and its rescue from the limbo of urban devastation to recognize its role as a part of the formal inhabited city. Designers need to engage with this infrastructural landscape: mundane parking facilities, difficult spaces under elevated roads, complex transit interchanges, and landscapes generated by waste processes.

(p. 171)

We concur, and in the second half of this book, our focus turns to how we might redesign four types of unremarkable spaces. Critically, we have purposely used the term space here – rather than place – as spaces become places when they are designed appropriately, with meaning (Cushing & Miller, 2020). As with the elements section above, we have organised these spaces according to the actions they accommodate:

Part 2: Five spaces

1) **Passing Under:** underpasses.
2) **Strolling Along:** streets and sidewalks.
3) **Going Places:** bikeways and multi-use trails.
4) **Staying Put:** parking lots.
5) **Spending Time and Money:** shopping centres.

Who should read this book?

The inhabitants and designers of our cities should read this book. If you live in an urban area, or even a suburban area, this book will give you a new perspective on the spaces you pass by and use daily. It will give you a new way to see your city and think about how you interpret it and interact with it. Landscape architecture, urban design, planning, industrial design, and architecture practitioners, academics, and students interested in the built environment should also read this book, along with researchers and students in the fields of geography, sociology, political science, behaviour economics, information technology, public health, and public administration. Although we reference theory and research throughout, we have specifically written this book to be less about the 'data' and more about how we use and create urban spaces and elements in different ways. We hope to question why things are done and challenge those of you who have a role in creating spaces to think differently about the unremarkable spaces. Those spaces that may not require the big ticket, show stopping design elements – but are none-the-less critical to designing a positive urban experience. This book should also interest policymakers and public managers who want to improve their understanding of the innovative design of 'unremarkable' elements and spaces, as we provide practical and context-specific insights, recommendations, and examples of innovative-best practice from cities around the world.

How to use this book

There are many different ways to use this book. If you are interested in the creative and unusual ways that designers, policymakers, and citizens are positively transforming their cities by redesigning unremarkable elements and spaces, then you can read the book from cover to cover. If you are interested in one specific feature of the built environment, and how that might be designed to be more sustainable, more salutogenic, and more playful, then you may choose to go straight to that chapter. Each chapter can stand alone, making it possible to jump around and read one chapter at a time and not in any particular order. We even encourage you to go back and re-read a chapter if it is of particular interest.

As you read this book, however, we encourage you to take a moment to reflect on the critically important task facing us – redesigning our urban form for the twenty-first century and beyond (Carmona et al., 2010). Like Adam Rogers, we believe 'a city shouldn't just happen anymore. Every block, every building, every brick represents innumerable decisions. Decide well, and cities are magic' (Rogers, 2015). These decisions are critical. And we hope this book can inspire a greater focus on the small details and design decisions about the everyday spaces and elements within the urban realm that are often taken for granted. And as we argued in *Creating Great Places*, it is no longer acceptable to design urban spaces that do not contribute to living healthier and happier lives. Each chapter here explores how conscious consideration of 'the unremarkable' might advance the key real-world urban trends and priorities of sustainable, salutogenic, and playful design.

Additionally, as we outline in the Appendix, you might also choose to use our theory storming approach (see Cushing & Miller, 2020; Miller & Cushing, 2021) to re-imagine the design of a street as biophilic or inclusive, for example. Theory storming approach is inspired, in part, by Edward de Bono's Six Thinking Hats (2007) approach – where wearers metaphorically put on a different coloured hat or perspective through which to approach a problem (e.g. putting on the yellow hat of optimism or the green hat of creativity). Theory storming approach encourages participants to critically approach design challenges and potential solutions through multiple theoretical lenses – for example, *affordance* theory, then *biophilia* theory, then *sense of place* theory, and so on, and is an explicit strategy to foster creative, generative, 'outside-the box' thinking.

Most importantly – enjoy this book!

Many of us live in urban environments or will soon. The statistics are familiar: by 2050, nearly 70% of the world's population will live in cities – from 751 million in 1950 to 4.2 billion in 2018 and 6.4 billion by 2050 (United Nations, 2018). We all have a stake in how our cities are designed. Whether we have a role in design decisions or are merely concerned with how our environment impacts our daily activities and can improve our health and well-being, the design of the unremarkable has an impact. This book challenges the way we see our urban environments, and the importance we place on those spaces and elements that are commonly only afterthoughts.

Notes

1 Read about the intervention here: https://www.keepbritaintidy.org/sites/default/files/resources/KBT_CFSI_Green_Footprints_Case_Study_2015.pdf
2 Visit https://www.playablecity.com/ to see case studies and videos and be inspired.

References

Beatley, T. (2016). *Handbook of biophilic city planning and design*. Island Press.

Brown, L., & Dixon, D. (2014). *Urban design for an urban century: Shaping more livable, equitable, and resilient cities* (2nd ed.). Wiley.

Carmona, M., Tiesdall, S., Heath, T., & Oc, T. (2010). *Public places, urban spaces: The dimensions of urban design* (2nd ed.). Architectural Press, Elsevier.

Crawley, J. (2010). Piano stairs art project – Options for music in public domain. *Future Melbourne Committee Report*. Retrieved 20 May 2019 from https://www.melbourne.vic.gov.au/about-council/committees-meetings/meeting-archive/MeetingAgendaItemAttachments/469/7567/6.2.pdf

Curl, A., Kearns, A. J., Macdonald, L., Mason, P., & Ellaway, A. (2018). Can walking habits be encouraged through area-based regeneration and relocation? A longitudinal study of deprived communities in Glasgow, UK. *Journal of Transportation & Health, 10*, 44–55.

Cushing, D., & Miller, E. (2020). *Creating great places: Evidence-based urban design for health and wellbeing*. Routledge.

de Bono, E. (2007). *Six thinking hats: An essential approach to business management*. Little, Brown & Company.

Douglas, G. (2018). *The help yourself city: Inequality and legitimacy in DIY urbanism*. Oxford University Press.

Egenhoefer, R. (2018). *Routledge handbook of sustainable design*. Routledge.

Finn, D. (2014). DIY urbanism: Implications for cities. *Journal of Urbanism: International Research on Placemaking and Urban Sustainability, 7*(4), 381–398.

Froehlich, J. (2015). Gamifying green: Gamification and environmental sustainability. In S. Walz & S. Deterding (Eds.), *The gameful world* (pp. 563–596). MIT Press.

Halliday, S. (2018). *Sustainable construction* (2nd ed.). Routledge.

Hancock, T., Capon, A. G., Dietrich, U., & Patrick, R. A. (2016). Governance for health in the Anthropocene. *International Journal of Health Governance*, 21(4), 245–262. https://doi.org/10.1108/IJHG-08-2016-0041

Hansen, P., & Jespersen, A. (2013). Nudge and the manipulation of choice. A framework for the responsible use of nudge approach to behaviour change in public policy. *European Journal of Risk Regulation*, 4(1), 3–28.

Holt-Lunstad, J., Smith, T., Baker, M., Harris, T., & Stephenson, D. (2015). Loneliness and social isolation as risk factors for mortality: A meta-analytic review. *Perspectives on Psychological Science*, 10(2), 227–237. https://doi.org/10.1177/1745691614568352

Hur, M., & Nasar, J. (2014). Physical upkeep, perceived upkeep, fear of crime and neighborhood satisfaction. *Journal of Environmental Psychology*, 38, 186–194.

Iveson, K. (2013). Cities within the city: Do-it-yourself urbanism and the right to the city. *International Journal of Urban and Regional Research*, 37(3), 941–956.

Jacobs, J. (1961). *The Death and Life of Great American Cities*. Random House.

Kelling, G., & Coles, C. (1996). *Fixing broken windows: Restoring order and reducing crime in our communities*. Simon and Schuster.

Lefebvre, H. (1968). *Le droit a la ville (The right to the city)*. Anthropos.

Lewin, K. (1936). *Principles of topological psychology*. McGraw-Hill Inc.

Medway, D., Parker, C., & Roper, S. (2016). Litter, gender and brand: The anticipation of incivilities and perceptions of crime prevalence. *Journal of Environmental Psychology*, 45, 135–144.

Miller, E., & Cushing, D. (2021). Theory-storming in the urban realm: Using nudge theory to inform the design of health-promoting places. *The Journal of Design Strategies*, 10(1), 112–121.

Mossop, E. (2006). *Contemporary Australian landscape design*. University of Technology Sydney.

Müller, B., & Shimizu, H. (2018). *Towards the implementation of the new urban agenda: Contributions from Japan and Germany to make cities more environmentally sustainable*. Springer.

Nassauer, J. (1995). Messy ecosystems, orderly frames. *Landscape Journal*, 14(2), 161–169.

Newman, P., Beatley, T., & Boyer, H. (2014). *Resilient cities: Responding to peak oil and climate change* (2nd ed.). Island Press.

Newsroom. (2015). *Edinburgh recycling rates soar 85 per cent*. Retrieved from https://www.edinburghnews.scotsman.com/news/edinburgh-recycling-rates-soar-85-cent-1516403

Nijholt, A. (2017). *Playable cities: The city as a digital playground*. Springer.

Nijholt, A. (2018). Playable cities for children (pp. 14–20). In Fukuda, S. (Ed). *Advances in affective and pleasurable design: Proceedings of the AHFE*. Springer.

Nijholt, A. (2020). Playful introduction on 'Making smart cities more playable.' In A. Nijholt (Ed.), *Making smart cities more playable exploring playable cities* (pp. 1–25). Springer.

O'Sullivan, F. (2016). *The problem with 'playable' cities*. Bloomberg. Retrieved from https://www.bloomberg.com/news/articles/2016-11-07/what-the-playable-cities-concept-gets-wrong

Rivera, M. B., Ringenson, T., & Pargman, D. (2020). The sustainable playable city: Making way for the playful citizen. In A. Nijholt (Ed.), *Making smart cities more playable: Gaming media and social effects* (pp. 87–106). Springer.

Rogers, A. (2015). *WIRED looks at 8 cities of the future.* Retrieved 10 June 2019 from https://www.archdaily.com/774965/wired-looks-at-8-cities-of-the-future

Roggema, R. (2022). *Design for regenerative cities and landscapes: Rebalancing human impact and natural environment.* Springer.

Thaler, R., & Sunstein, C. (2008). *Nudge: Improving decisions about health, wealth and happiness.* Yale University Press.

Thomson, G., & Newman, P. (2018). Urban fabrics and urban metabolism—From sustainable to regenerative cities. *Resources, Conversation and Recycling, 132,* 218–229.

Tonkiss, F. (2014). *Cities by design: The social life of urban form.* Polity Press.

United Nations. (2018). *Revisions of world urbanization prospects.* Retrieved 7 May 2019 from https://www.un.org/development/desa/en/news/population/2018-revision-of-world-urbanization-prospects.html

Weissbourd, R., Batanova, M., Lovison, V., & Torres, E. (2021). *Loneliness in America how the pandemic has deepened an epidemic of loneliness and what we can do about it?* Retrieved from https://mcc.gse.harvard.edu/reports/loneliness-in-america

Wheeler, S. (2013). *Planning for sustainability: Creating livable, equitable and ecological communities* (2nd ed.). Routledge.

Wilson, J., & Kelling, G. (1982). Broken windows: The police and neighborhood safety. *Atlantic Monthly, 211,* 29–38.

Zhou, S. (2021). Contested suburban mobilities: Towards a sustainable urbanism of justice and difference. In S. Ryder, K. Powlen, M. Laituri, S. Malin, J. Sbicca, & D. Stevios (Eds.), *Environmental justice in the Anthropocene: From (un)just presents to just futures* (pp. 215–229). Routledge.

Section I

Unremarkable elements

2 Throwing out

Redesigning trash bins and landfills to be more remarkable

We start our exploration of 'unremarkable' elements of the built environment by focusing on an important yet mundane and frequently overlooked everyday process: waste management, specifically the design of trash bins and landfills. Soon forgotten by those who produce it, waste is magically transported 'away' to unimagined, ignored, and marginalised places, with most people rarely pondering the process of waste disposal or the potential significance of rubbish bin design.

As a society, we produce a lot of waste. The statistics tell us that, on average, people create an average of 0.74 kilogram of waste each day, ranging from 0.11 to 4.54 kilograms (World Bank, 2022). In 2017, Americans threw out over 267.8 million tonnes of 'municipal solid waste' or an average of 4.51 pounds (~2 kg) per day per person. Despite decades of public information campaigns on reducing, reusing, and recycling, half of all materials discarded by homes and businesses is dumped in landfills, with only a third recycled or composted (52.1% vs. 35.2%; EPA, 2020).

The creative arts have been used to trigger reflection and change our waste behaviours. In 2008, Greenpeace[1] released a catchy rap song, *Buy it, Use it, Break it, Junk it, it's Toxic*, while filmmaker Annie Leonard's short 22-minute animated documentary in 2009, *The Story of Stuff*, memorably illuminated the lifecycle of material goods and the problems of our linear system of extraction, production, distribution, consumption, and disposal. More recently, Gregg Segal's *7 Days of Garbage*[2] photographic series shows Americans surrounded by a week's worth of household rubbish, while waste activist Jacquelyn Ottman (2019) has crafted a thought-provoking poem – reproduced below – to challenge us to think differently and take responsibility for the trash we personally create.

The Girls with the Jars
I'm always amazed at those 'zero waste'
girls with their mason jars. And their
big proclamations: Here is all the trash
I generated last year!

DOI: 10.4324/9781003052746-3

> Inside each jar is usually a tiny jum-
> ble of twist'ems from the broccoli, a few
> of those little plastic tabs that keep the
> bread bags tight, and a colourful array of
> produce stickers.
> Although I'm a bit skeptical, I do appre-
> ciate that they give a damn. And I thank
> them for making me think.
>
> What if at the end of every year we all
> had to show the world how much trash
> we created?
>
> Would we shout so loudly?
> How big a jar would we need?
> Jacquelyn Ottman

In this chapter, we look at the experience of waste management from a very different lens, asking how we might redesign trash bins and landfills through the lens of sustainable and playable design. Despite a significant amount of literature documenting trash and recycling behaviours *inside* the home (e.g. Comber & Thieme, 2012), much less attention has been paid to the design and use of waste systems *outside* the home – the public spaces in our urban environment, including parks, playgrounds, shopping centres, streets, schools, railway, and bus stations, as well as the more neglected spaces of waste disposal and recycling sites. Drawing on both existing and speculative opportunities for inspiration, this chapter focuses on how we might redesign these public sites of waste disposal to be more remarkable.

A brief history of waste – and the vision for a waste-free world

The systematic and scientific study of modern-day trash, and the patterns and processes of waste creation and disposal, is known as garbology (Rathje & Murphy, 2001). Throughout history, humans have always generated waste and responded in very different ways to waste management. For thousands of years, waste was simply thrown out of windows and doors, with these large piles of stinking waste causing health and transportation challenges. In 500 BC, Athens in Greece organised the first municipal dump in the western world, regulating that waste must be dumped at least a mile from city limits. Few cities followed this practice and it was not until the 1300s that the French made it a legal requirement to have a municipal dump, and the English made it illegal to dump waste in public waterways and ditches.

The mismanagement of waste in cities negatively impacted the quality of urban life. In the 1880s, reports linking disease to filthy environments triggered 'the age of sanitation' and a significant advance in public health, with waste and drainage systems constructed to remove sewage. Early garbage removal trucks were open-bodied dump trucks, pulled by horses, while several American cities used pigs to dispose of the garbage. With the increasing urbanisation of the population and concentration of waste, by the 1920s, landfills were the most popular method (Friis, 2012).

Today, landfills remain the cornerstone of the waste management system. These large-scale government waste disposal systems are hidden, invisible, and disconnected from people, promoting denial and abstraction (Hawkins, 2006; Muller, 2016). Most people do not like to think or talk about where our trash goes, with landscape architect Mira Engler (2004) memorably labelling landfills, sewage treatment plants, waste disposal, and recycling sites as *'waste landscapes'*. Landfills and trash bins have, traditionally, been designed to hide from us the evidence of our consumption – and with our waste hidden, as a global society, we typically fail to notice, think about or act on waste (Chappells & Shove, 1999; Engler, 2004).

How we view and manage waste is, slowly, changing. Contemporary waste management strategies argue that we must transition from our inefficient and wasteful linear economy with a 'take-make-consume-dispose' pattern, to a circular economy where waste is viewed as a resource and designed out or reused through a closed-loop approach. Perhaps the most memorable example of closed-loop recycling rubbish bins is the Gumdrop bin, as illustrated in Figure 2.1. These bright pink bins – designed to collect waste chewing gum – look like strawberry flavoured bubble gum bubbles and are made from waste chewing gum. Gumdrop bins collect discarded chewing gum, which is then recycled and processed to become gumboots, mobile phone covers, stationery, packaging, and most recently, the sole of Adidas's iconic Stan Smith shoe. The Gumdrop Bin Schools Programme launched a gum litter campaign, *'What Will Your Gum Become'* across the United Kingdom to inspire school students to think about what can be created when they dispose of their chewing gum correctly. With the motto of SHAKE, MAKE & CREATE, the campaign encourages students to 'SHAKE their littering habits whilst helping to MAKE a difference, and subsequently CREATE new products' (Gumdrop, 2022).

Chewing gum recycling bins are just the beginning of a much-needed transition to a more sustainable society, with the European Union (EU) identifying turning waste into a resource as key to meeting their 2050 vision of 'living well, within the limits of the planet'. The vision presented in the EU's Roadmap to a Resource Efficient Europe has motivated Wales for example, to commit to reducing food waste

32 Unremarkable elements

Figure 2.1 A gumdrop bin, on an urban street.
Credit: Gumdrop.

by 50% and setting a recycling target for municipal waste of 80% – which will impact our relationship with waste and the design of rubbish systems (European Environment Agency, 2020). The European Environment Agency's R-ladder outlines the following key steps in the waste reduction process: refusing, rethinking, reducing, reusing, repairing, refurbishing, remanufacturing, repurposing, recycling, and recovering (2020, p. 85). Success in this waste reduction journey will mean confronting decades of unsustainable consumption patterns and built in obsolescence (O'Connor, 2019), with the thoughtful redesign of bins and landfills one component of a much needed transition to a waste-free world.

Of course, we acknowledge that behaviour and habit change, especially litter behaviour is complex. A wealth of behaviour change literature, from social psychology, sociology, human-computer interaction (HCI), landscape architecture, and urban planning, has explored the determinants of waste-related attitudes and sustainability actions from the lens of the Theory of Planned Behavior and Value-Belief-Norm

Theory (Kollmuss & Agyeman, 2002). These studies highlight that promotion and education alone is not enough to change behaviours, with issues of convenience, cost, rewards, and social norms critical. Additionally, as Prestina and Pearce (2010) explain, infrastructure is key for recycling to become a habit as it, 'is not enough for recycling infrastructure to be present at some times in some places—it must be consistently available' (p. 1023). As argued throughout this book, the creative quality of often neglected elements and features of our built environment infrastructure – that is, whether it is designed to be remarkable or unremarkable – has a critical and under-explored role to play in our transition towards a more sustainable planet.

Proposition 1: Redesigning bins to nudge sustainable behaviours

Our first proposition in this chapter is that public trash bins, the most visible reminder of waste in our public realm, can and should be redesigned to nudge sustainable behaviours. Bin design has evolved from one large metal bin to include options for recycling, typically offering separate containers and slots for compostable and recyclable items, such as bottles, cans, plastics, metals, and newspapers. The physical design features of the bin, from the location, placement, height, size, and number of containers and slots, act as what Norman (2013) terms 'forcing functions', processes that 'force' a person to do the right thing which in this context is to appropriately dispose of litter. The growing presence of recycling options in bin designs also serves as an affordance, a visual cue that tells the user what to do. Consider, for example, the design of coffee cup recycling bins popping up across the globe. People are often confused about whether coffee cups are recyclable, or what components are; providing clear signage and shaped components for recycling cups and lids separately signals the action to take.

Nudging bin use and sustainability through humorous graphic design

Despite significant investment, environmentally friendly messaging, social marketing, and advertising encouraging people to engage in sustainable behaviours is often not successful. In response, a handful of researchers have recently advocated for the use of humour, arguing that when fear exists – such as around the environment – humour is a strategy that leverages positive emotions to foster interactive engagement and action (Brennan et al., 2020; Griese et al., 2018). Lister et al.'s (2015) laugh model in health promotion, for example, purposely uses humour, engagement, and entertainment to connect

Figure 2.2 Public trash bin where graphic design uses humour to nudge sustainability.
Credit: Kristin Hardy Design.

audiences with programmes and provoke simple actions. Humour often works through surprise, which we see in the messaging on public trash bins depicted in Figure 2.2.

The El Cajon Boulevard Business Improvement Association in San Diego commissioned graphic designer Kristen Hardy to stencil art onto the sides of trash and recycle bins. Hardy used art deco humour to prompt recycling as we see in Figure 2.2, with the quote on the side of one recycling bin reading, '*I'm not trashy my dear, I recycle*'. This thoughtful humorous messaging, combined with clean design aesthetic, encourages passers-by to pause and rethink the simple action of rubbish disposal. Similarly, in Small, Spain, large speech bubbles have been installed on beaches saying, '*I'm a beach not an enormous ashtray, ok?*'.

Thoughtful graphic design and messaging might also positively nudge the use of recycling bins. One recent study at a festival revealed that bins under motivational signs, '*95% of people get it right—can you?; it's easy being green; help save the planet*, elicited a greater amount of waste. Unfortunately, waste was no better sorted in these bins than those located under the baseline sign. However, the research team did observe more *conversations* about waste disposal behaviour under the motivational signs, with participants noting, '*oh no we were both wrong*' or '*oh look we got it right*' (Verdonk et al., 2017). Such thoughts are an example of what Donald Schön (1983) labels, '*reflection-in-action*', the analysis of behaviour *as it occurs*, and can be an important trigger for reflection and future behaviour change.

A handful of studies have also explored if and how 'watching eyes', a reminder of social norms, might influence littering behaviour. Francey and Bergmuller (2012) explored if the design of a trash bin – one with and one without a picture of eyes – might affect how people responded to litter left at a bus stop bench. The presence of eyes did not actually increase the likelihood people would pick up litter but did positively influence the amount of time spent: people who cleaned up the bench spent more time doing so when the bin had eyes on it. Interestingly, the visual image of eyes – and the subtle cue that your behaviour is being observed by others – appears to be more important than an explicit anti-littering message. For example, in an experimental study exploring littering in a university cafeteria, Ernest-Jones et al. (2011) halved the odds of littering in the presence of posters featuring eyes versus posters featuring flowers, regardless of whether the poster advocated litter clearing or an unrelated message.

Nudging bin use by engaging communities in the design process

New York City has actively engaged the public in rethinking bin design with the Better Bin[3] design competition launched in 2019 to reimagine the 23,000 green wire mesh litter baskets that have lined the streets of New York since the 1930s. The competition brief called for a 'practical and efficient litter basket … that reduces litter and better serves both Sanitation Workers and the public'. There was a focus on ergonomics, acknowledging that full bins are very heavy to move and empty, and that the current drainage system which lets rainwater and fluids flow through and out, needed to be maintained.

There were 200 submissions from six continents, with two finalist teams selected to produce and test 12 full-size prototype baskets in three New York City neighbourhoods over 90 days, gathering feedback from both the public and sanitation workers. The winning design, from Group Project, featured an interior liner that was nearly 50% lighter with eight comfortable grips, compared to two in the existing design, for proper lifting. What is notable here is that the redesign of something quite unremarkable, a public trash bin, became a project that engaged residents in a conversation about design, ergonomics, sustainability, and consumption. Waste, and its management, was made visible.

Globally, cities are experimenting with *transparent rubbish bins* to make waste behaviours more visible. A trial in Halifax, Nova Scotia, for example, found that transparent rubbish bins decreased the portion of garbage sent to landfill by a third. Other cities are generating income from trash bins, adding large digital screens to their side, and selling this space to display local events, advertisements, weather, and public transport status information. Imagine however, if the display of bins conveyed similar information, perhaps reporting on local recycling behaviours to make the cities' daily waste footprint more visible, or using the Internet of Things to model, visualise, and control garbage collection.

Nudging bin use through digital, virtual, and augmented reality technologies

When it comes to the intentional design of public trash bins, the small number of projects come from HCI researchers. Here, bins have been connected to technology with researchers using interactive displays, social media, feedback, and habit disrupting cues such as buzzes, beeps, texts, and light signals to encourage trash disposal and recycling behaviour. BinCam, for example, is a smart recycle bin that informs household users' social network about their recycling behaviour – whenever the lid opens and closes, images of the thrown-away items is posted online to Facebook. Conscious of the ethical and privacy concerns, Thieme et al. (2012) designed this project to be a trigger for reflection on household waste behaviours.

Only a handful of projects have focused on public bins. Over a decade ago, noting that urban trash is often 'ignored or regarded as disgusting' yet 'reveals fascinatingly rich details of urban life', Paulos and Jenkins (2005, p. 344) investigated how people used a central trash can in downtown San Francisco. The trash can was used every 80 seconds, with a minimum of five seconds and maximum of six minutes between interactions. Paulos and Jenkins (2006) then created a functional augmented trash can – *Jetsam* – designed to expose city dwellers to the pattern of trash interactions. An overhead camera recorded the top layer of trash, a digital scale measured its weight, and a computer and projector continually displayed an animated image of the trash items onto the pavement.

The resulting visualisation was a layering of trash can activities and patterns, with 'trash images' slowing progressing outward, sorted by weight and time, eventually disappearing. People could interact with the augmented trash can in active, passive, and mobile ways; tossing trash in was active, while anybody passing by and observing the shifting visualization was a passive participant. Paulos and Jenkins also envisioned mobile interactions, including a text message sent to a piece of trash or integrated into the display as street poetry, or an interaction whereby the person would be sent back a recycling statistic. While such visualisations of trash are not yet commonplace, such initiatives are an unusual and engaging way to start a conversation about waste, enabling 'visualizations of patterns, flows, and prompt further reflection on urban trash, its value, and usage' (Paulos & Jenkins, 2005, p. 350).

HCI researchers have also looked at how augmented recycling bins might positively impact recycling behaviours. Compared to a standard bottle recycling bin installed in a university lobby, Berengueres et al.'s (2013) 'emoticon-bin' prototype, a recycle bin which rewards users with smiles and sounds created using an LCD screen, proximity sensor and speakers, increased the recycling rate threefold. Anthropomorphic recycling bins turn the trash bin into something users can relate to, mimicking human or animal appearances. In Japan, Yamaji et al. (2011) designed a trash robot – the Sociable Trash Box– which walks towards trash and encourages children to pick it up. The Sociable Trash Box is a small round trash bin with an eye (camera), small floppy arms, and the ability to turn around, bow, and walk, with the aim of obtaining 'child-assistance in collecting trash from a public space, while establishing a social interaction between the child and robot' (Yamaji et al., 2011, p. 360). The Sociable Trash Box engages with twisting and bowing motions when children put trash into the container. We need more of these studies to show us if and how the creative use of technology and interactive bins might reduce littering, enhance recycling, and contribute to a waste-free world.

Proposition 2: Nudging bin use and rethinking landfills through playable design

Our second proposition argues that we must make engaging with bins – and landfills – more fun, by applying principles of playable design. Perhaps the most well-known example of the gamification of rubbish and 'playable bins' comes from the German car company Volkswagen's Fun Theory campaign, which aimed to make responsible behaviour more fun. The public proposed ideas and the best ideas were built. One outcome was '*the world's deepest bin*' when you drop trash into the bin, it plays an extended falling sound,[4] and '*bottle bank arcade*' which turned a bottle recycling bin into a video game-like challenge (see King & Chang, 2016). While Volkswagen's Fun Theory campaign resulted in one off interventions, a handful of HCI researchers, activists, and designers are using persuasive, playful technologies to influence people's waste disposal behaviours.

Globally, there are many local tech versions of turning litter disposal into a game. The city of Lucerne in Switzerland created 16 game stations[5] including a maze and a large painted hopscotch around public bins to raise awareness about the importance of keeping city streets free of trash, applying playable design principles to make the process more enjoyable. Many cities paint the pavement in front of bins to create small basketball courts, turning the bin into a basket. High schools increasingly hang basketball hoops above recycling and rubbish bins, and chalk out a 'free throw line' to encourage students to throw their trash into a bin, instead of littering.

A charity focused on designing campaigns that inspire environmentally friendly lifestyles, Hubbub UK, has engaged with nudge theory and playable design to encourage the appropriate disposal of cigarette butts. Figure 2.3 shows the Ballot Bin (from $A500) – the world's

Unremarkable elements

Figure 2.3 The world's first voting ashtray.
Credit: Hubbub UK.

first voting ashtray. The smoker 'votes' by putting their cigarette butt in the slots underneath their preferred answer to create a visible public opinion poll, as the old butts pile up. Magnetic letters mean the question can be changed regularly, with the Ballot Bin said to reduce cigarette butt litter by 46%. By designing creative bins and making the typically mundane act of litter disposal more fun, Hubbub UK is working to create a 'culture of recycling on the go'.

Australian design firm Sencity[6] has created TetraBIN®, using gamified digital technologies to make disposing of rubbish fun. Using the latest in LED media façade technology and infrared sensors, disposing trash in the bin starts a colourful Tetris game, with the pattern of the blocks determined by the size and shape of the litter. The bin can be set to different Nintendo-style games, meaning that by disposing of litter you can feed a dog a bone, or 'push' Tetris-like blocks into position. The creators are working on enabling customised messaging and informal polling, which means that people could – for example – vote for their sports team by tossing litter into one slot. TetraBIN® illustrates how engaging with a playable design mindset can transform a mundane activity – disposing of rubbish – into something fun.

While only a few of us are smokers, we all wear clothes – and the challenge of fast fashion and textile waste is a significant problem. Fashion labels and clothing stories are increasingly utilising circular economy approaches to manage textile waste (see Chapter 10 which features a mall that sells only recycled products), with H & M offering an in-store garment collection programme where customers can drop off a bag of unwanted clothes in return for a 15% discount. And Bosch and Kanis (2013), working with game, interaction, and fashion designers, as well as textile and fashion sustainability experts, designed a playful textile recycling machine targeted at young adults – university students. Iterative prototypes included rewards – music and confetti from the bin opening, feedback on the impact of their decision to recycle – balloons that signalled how much oil, water, and carbon dioxide they had saved, and a hologram machine – discarded due to lighting and scaling challenges. Bosch and Kanis found that university students responded best when the container did something unexpected, and so the final system, UNI-BIN, played sounds and animations illustrating the textile recycling and production processes. UNI-BIN also gave users tickets to track their own contributions, and in-line with a closed-loop recycling process, their donated textile materials were turned into an upcycled fashion line.

Nudging the playable design of landfills, through hedonistic sustainability

Landfills can also be designed differently, with sustainability and play in mind, as we see in Figure 2.4. The CopenHill project in Copenhagen,

Figure 2.4 CopenHill in Copenhagen, Denmark –site of waste, park, and ski slope. Credit: Bjarke Ingles Group, photographer Rasmus-Hjortshoj.

Denmark, is an extremely innovative example of a playable and sustainable approach to managing waste. CopenHill, an incinerator that burns waste to produce heat and electricity, is the cleanest waste-to-energy power plant in the world – and on the roof is a large human-made mountain that serves as a public park and artificial ski slope, with tree lined hiking trails and the tallest artificial climbing wall in the world on the facade. This innovative design turns a typically unused feature of a building, the roof, into a resource for the local community, a park with a sustainability education centre inside as well.

The original design from the Bjarke Ingles Group also turned the 124 metre high chimney into an artwork that would emit a ring of vapour every time 250 kilograms of carbon dioxide is released into the atmosphere, visibly reminding residents of their carbon footprint and the result of consumption and waste. While that feature of the project has not been realised, the innovative design – where the façade is climbable, roof hikeable, and slopes skiable – embodies Danish architect Bjarke Ingels' vision of 'hedonistic sustainability', where a sustainable city is better for both the environment and makes day-to-day life more enjoyable for residents, an approach which resonates with playable design. Leading such innovative projects is not without challenge however, with Bjarke Ingels recalling how his CEO called him up and said, '*Bjarke, this is a $1 billion project in our hometown. We want to win this. Don't fuck it up with a ski slope*' (Chu, 2015).

As we start to think differently about our relationship with waste management systems, CopenHill illustrates the value of thinking and designing through the lens of both sustainable and playable design, and raises the proposition that perhaps our transition towards a more sustainable future might be quicker if more designers adopted Ingels 'hedonistic sustainability'[7] vision, that sustainability can and should be pleasurable.

Making our waste system more visible, sustainable, and playable, by design

If we are to successfully transition towards a more sustainable world, we must think very differently about waste management and the design of bins and landfills. Art making and creating is a powerful tool for engaging the public in this much-needed dialogue, with the work of American artist Mierle Ukeles particularly inspiring. Since 1977, Ukeles has been an unsalaried artist in residence at the New York City Department of Sanitation. In this self-initiated role, Ukeles uses art to draw attention to the low cultural status of maintenance work and to give the public a deeper understanding of the waste collection system. Her 'Flow City' exhibition (1983–1990), installed at a recycling plant in New York City, gave the public unprecedented insight into waste management process, and what happens '*between the trash they put to the curb for the garbage man to collect, and the aggregate mass of trash produced by everyone in the city and the labor required to deal with it*' (Muller, 2016, p. 20).

In San Francisco, a unique Artist in Residence Program has provided local artists since 1990, a four-month residency offering a stipend, access to discarded materials, and a studio space at Recology, the Recycling and Transfer Center, which is also home to a three-acre sculpture garden containing work by former artists in residence. The residency ends with a three-day exhibition, with the artists also teaching the public about recycling and resource conservation.

Conclusion

Whether it is turning trash into art, designing landfills to also be ski-fields, creating chewing gum recycling bins, or turning rubbish bins into a place for basketball, this chapter has identified a small and growing number of exemplar people, projects, and products designed to transform what is often mundane and unremarkable (bins and landfills) into attractive features of our urban environment that nudge sustainability and play. Of course, we acknowledge that the desired end objective is to embrace circular economy principles and reduce the amount of waste we generate, through a closed-loop approach of restorative and regenerative design. And as Jacquelyn Ottman (2019) reminds us in her poem below, if we would simply change our mindset, we would realise that our trash is, in fact, often treasure.

One minute to the next

One minute, it's trash
The next minute, it's treasure
All it takes is one person plucking an
item from the trash
and deciding to take it home.
Jacquelyn Ottman

In the next chapter, we continue our exploration of the unremarkable – and how we might thoughtfully redesign it – by turning our attention to public seating.

Notes

1 Watch the rap here: https://www.youtube.com/watch?v=4mLtheejM30
2 To see these images, visit: https://www.greggsegal.com/P-Projects/7-Days-of-Garbage/6/caption
3 BetterBin (betterbin.nyc) was the inaugural competition in the Van Alen

Institute's product Placed initiative, a series of design competitions geared to improve urban life that was a collaboration with the Department of Sanitation, the Industrial Designers Society of America and the American Institute of Architects New York.

4 Watch a video here: https://www.youtube.com/watch?v=qRgWttqFKu8
5 See: https://scene360.com/design/18997/game-incentives-to-stop-littering/#:~:text=In%20the%20city%20of%20Lucerne,maze%2C%20hopscotch%20and%20other%20activities
6 Find out more here: https://sencity.city/tetrabin
7 Watch his TED talk here: https://www.ted.com/talks/bjarke_ingels_hedonistic_sustainability

References

Berengueres, J., Alsuwairi, F., Zaki, N., & Ng, T. (2013). Gamification of a recycle bin with emoticons. In *8th ACM/IEEE International Conference on Human-Robot Interaction* (HRI) (pp. 83–84).

Bosch, L., & Kanis, M. (2013). Encouraging sustainable fashion with a playful recycling system. In *Proceedings of the 27th International BCS Human Computer Interaction Conference* (Article 46, pp. 1–6).

Brennan, L., Parker, L., Nguyen, D., & Pochun, T. (2020). Positive emotions in social marketing and social advertising using humor. In L. Parker & L. Brennan (Eds.), *Social marketing and advertising in the age of social media* (pp. 102–119). Edward Elgar.

Chappells, E., & Shove, E. (1999). The dustbin: A study of domestic waste, household practices and utility services. *International Planning Studies*, *4*, 267–280.

Chu, J. (2015). Bjarke Ingels on the future of architecture. *Fast Company*, https://www.fastcompany.com/3041276/bjarke-ingels-on-the-future-of-architecture

Comber, R., & Thieme, A. (2012). Designing beyond habit: Opening space for improved recycling and food waste behaviors through processes of persuasion, social influence and aversive affect. *Personal and Ubiquitous Computing*, *17*(6), 1197–1210.

Engler, M. (2004). *Designing America's waste landscapes*. John Hopkins University Press.

Environmental Protection Agency (EPA). (2020). *Facts and figures about materials, waste and recycling*. Retrieved from https://www.epa.gov/facts-and-figures-about-materials-waste-and-recycling/national-overview-facts-and-figures-materials

Ernest-Jones, M., Nettle, D., & Bateson, M. (2011). Effects of eye images on everyday cooperative behavior: A field experiment. *Evolution and Human Behavior*, *32*(3), 172–178.

European Environment Agency. (2020). *Resource efficiency and the circular economy in Europe 2019 – Even more from less: An overview of the policies, approaches and targets of 32 European countries*. European Environment Agency, Denmark.

Francey, D., & Bergmuller, R. (2012). Images of eyes enhance investments in a real-life public good. *PLoS ONE*, *7*(6), e37397.

Friis, R. (2012). Solutions to the growing waste problem. In R. H. Friis (Ed.), *The Praeger handbook of environmental health* (pp. 197–214). Praeger.

Griese, K.-M., Alexandrov, A., Michaelis, C., & Lilly, B. (2018). Examining the effect of humor in environmentally-friendly advertising. *Marketing Management Journal*, *28*(1), 30–47.

Gumdrop. (2022). *Gumdrop*. https://gumdropltd.com

Hawkins, G. (2006). *The ethics of waste: How we relate to rubbish*. Rowman & Littlefield/University of New South Wales Press.

King, S., & Chang, K. (2016). *Understanding industrial design: Principles for UX and interaction design*. O'Reilly Media.

Kollmuss, A., & Agyeman, J. (2002). Mind the gap: Why do people act environmentally and what are the barriers to pro-environmental behavior? *Environmental Education Research*, *8*(3), 239–260.

Lister, C., Royne, M., Payne, H. E., Cannon, B., Hanson, C., & Barnes, M. (2015). The laugh model: Reframing and rebranding public health through social media. *American Journal of Public Health*, *105*(11), 2245–2251.

Muller, J. (2016). *The architecture of waste: Creating new avenues for public engagement with trash* [PhD thesis]. University of Maryland.

Norman, D. A. (2013). *The design of everyday things*. Basic Books.

O'Connor, F. (2019). Circular thinking in design: Reflections over 25 years' experience. In M. Charter (Ed.), *Designing for the circular economy*. Routledge.

Ottman, J. (2019). *If trash could talk: Poems, stories, and musings*. CreateSpace Independent Publishing.

Paulos, E., & Jenkins, T. (2005). Urban probes: Encountering our emerging urban atmospheres. *Proceedings of CHI* (pp. 341–350).

Paulos, E., & Jenkins, T. (2006). Jetsam: exposing our everyday discarded objects. *Demo Ubicomp'06*.

Prestina, A., & Pearce, K. (2010). We care a lot: Formative research for a social marketing campaign to promote school-based recycling. *Resources, Conservation and Recycling*, *54*, 1017–1026.

Rathje, W. L., & Murphy, C. (2001). *Rubbish!: The archaeology of garbage*. University of Arizona Press.

Schön, D. A. (1983). *The reflective practitioner: How professionals think in action*. Basic Books.

Thieme, A., Comber, R., Miebach, J., Weeden, J., Krämer, N., Lawson, S., & Olivier, P. (2012). We've bin watching you: Designing for reflection and social persuasion to promote sustainable lifestyles. In *Conference on Human Factors in Computing Systems – Proceedings*. doi/10.1145/2207676.2208394.

Verdonk, S., Chiveralls, K., & Dawson, D. (2017). Getting wasted at WOMADelaide: The effect of signage on waste disposal. *Sustainability*, *9*(3), 344–361.

World Bank. (2022). *Trends in solid waste management*. World Bank.

Yamaji, Y., Miyake, T., Yoshiike, Y., Silva, P. & Okada, M. (2011). STB: Child-dependent sociable trash box. *International Journal of Social Robotics*, *3*, 359–370.

3 Sitting down

Redesigning benches and chairs to be more remarkable

Public seating can be one of the key features of a place. In the opening scene of the movie *Forest Gump*, for example, the actor Tom Hanks sits on a park bench at a bus stop with his box of chocolates and suitcase, telling a story to a stranger. Spy movies and political dramas have used benches to set the scene for government agents or journalists receiving envelopes with incriminating evidence from their informants. Benches in parks or secluded places are used by people down on their luck who need a place to sleep, or people who want to spend their time feeding birds or watching people. You can find them along walking and jogging trails as places to rest, or for more athletic people to do a few push-ups or stretch their hamstrings. A bench is often perched at the top of a hill or on an overlook with an incredible view. And sometimes William H. Whyte's satirical observation rings true: 'benches are artefacts, the purpose of which is to punctuate architectural photographs' (Whyte, 1980, p. 33).

Often anthropomorphised and referred to as the 'humble' public bench (Green, 2013), the bench is a design element that is pervasive in our culture. Interestingly, the term 'bench' is also common in the English language with cultural references, be it bodybuilders comparing how much they can *bench*press; the *bench*warmer on the baseball team who suddenly gets to play; a full *bench* in the courtroom with multiple judges; or the *bench*marks we set to measure success. The term bench has many meanings.

Benches, and other forms of public seating, can contribute to the design of a place and take on many different styles. The possibilities are numerous, from timber picnic tables to wrought iron café style tables and chairs, from sculptural pieces to short seating walls, and from bench swings to bean bags, to simple blankets on a grass lawn. The provision and design of outdoor seating has a very significant impact on the look, feel, and experience of a space. Seating can be used to reinforce the theme of a singular design, as with book-shaped seating at a library. Or there can be a consistent style across an entire

DOI: 10.4324/9781003052746-4

city to support its identity, as with the iconic carriage green benches in Paris, attributed to architect Gabriel Davioud (Charleton, 2022; Guernier, n.d.).

As a critical element within urban space, seating is linked to other social and physical behaviours, and can enable other activities to occur. When people are out and about in cities, they need places to stop and rest, to wait for something or someone, to eat, to read or learn something, or to watch the world go by. If we want people to spend time in public spaces, we need to provide effective seating. Again, to quote Whyte, 'People tend to sit where there are places to sit' (Whyte, 1980, p. 28).

Seating can also contribute to a sense of community. 'A public seat, considered as a small place for meaningful human experience, can become the seed that generates community, and as such a significant and powerful tool for placemaking' (Legge, 2020, p. 443). Providing seating in a purposeful and thoughtful way can send important messages to people that they are allowed and encouraged to sit and be part of a place.

Despite the importance of seating, little thought is often put into its design. Poorly designed public seats are uncomfortable, offer little protection from the weather, and are not always located in appropriate locations. And in many cases, seating is absent from public spaces. The title of a *New York Times Magazine* opinion piece by Jonathan Lee (2021) sums it up, 'The Park Bench is an Endangered Species: In a world that wants you to pay for everything, public seating is becoming a luxury'. Lee writes, 'If a park bench is not being removed, the backup plan is often to make it uncomfortable. "Hostile architecture" — an urban design strategy intended to impede "anti-social" behavior — is proliferating all over the world' (Lee, 2021, p. 1). If this is true, it undermines the sentiments of Legge (2020), who refers to the provision of public seating as 'an opportunity to enhance urban equality, amenity, and to build social connections and community wellbeing' (p. 439).

This chapter considers how innovative solutions for outdoor seating are critical to creating great places that are more sustainable, salutogenic, and playable. Using several exemplars, we look at the act of 'sitting down' within the context of these three priorities, in order to inspire new ways of affording this common behaviour in the urban realm.

The importance of seating in public space

As we write this book, we are still adjusting to the challenges presented by the COVID-19 global pandemic, a scenario most of us had never contemplated or imagined before, other than in sci-fi movies. Many countries and communities have experienced lockdowns or have

46   Unremarkable elements

enforced strict social distancing rules to slow its transmission. Although many public spaces remained open during this time, people were no longer allowed to gather in large groups or felt comfortable socialising within these spaces. Most large gatherings had been cancelled or were at risk of becoming superspreader events. Public seating was often restricted to every other seat to help enforce social distancing. This phenomenon warrants careful consideration and planning because regardless of social distancing rules and comfort levels, humans will always need to sit and rest. And we know that seating, if designed appropriately, can be used for multiple reasons. That is unlikely to change.

The role of benches and public seating was highlighted during the peak of COVID. In a viewpoint piece published online for British VOGUE, Stoppard (2020) reflected on the unexpected importance of the park bench during COVID lockdowns in London, writing, 'Now, more than ever, a park bench is a stage set, a backdrop, a place for drama to play out. All over the city, people are arguing, getting together, admitting something terrible, passing on a good secret, declaring their love, betraying someone's trust'. The social connections that a park bench can afford are actually quite extensive, yet also quite simple. Having a space to sit and observe or hold a conversation can be significant.

Historically, public seating was critical to enable and enhance civic culture. Research on the use of benches in Florence, Italy, in the fourteenth and fifteenth centuries describes how stone benches were much more than just public seating, they represented an opportunity to engage in civic life (Elet, 2002). Despite their importance, 'social historians have barely touched on the functional use of benches, and the semiotic significance of the bench in the context of urban space has been entirely overlooked' (p. 444).

Seating has always played an important role in the sociability of a public space, a concept often considered a key principle of placemaking (PPS.org, n.d.). Discussing that role, Legge (2020) suggests that 'the ability, and the explicit welcome, to sit improves the sociability, safety, and success of the larger environment, essentially transforming it from an open space to a human-centric place' (p. 440). To afford opportunities for social connections, seating is a key component that gives people the chance to connect with others, at an intimate scale. Although these opportunities for social connections are critical, 'sitting' itself is now associated with negative implications in terms of physical activity and being active.

Why seating is critical for being active outside

Sitting is getting a bad rap. Labelled as 'the new smoking', media outlets use this tagline to get our attention. Of course, increased time sitting has health implications that shouldn't be ignored. If sitting means long periods in front of a screen, and a reduction in physical activity, then it is important to counteract the impact. And if it means sitting with bad posture, or in an uncomfortable position for long periods, it can cause long-term issues and eventually damage. Prolonged periods of sitting can cause back pain and stress on the back, neck, arms, and legs.[1]

Yet, realistically sitting is not the equivalent of smoking when it comes to direct health effects (Vallance et al., 2018). Our increasingly common desk jobs and our addiction to screens exacerbate the habit of too much sitting. Binge-watching Netflix on the couch is more to blame than our use of benches in public space. Nevertheless, we need to design spaces to consider current lifestyles, habits, and needs.

For older adults, benches and public seating can be critical to feeling confident enough to walk outside in their neighbourhood, knowing they may need to stop and rest. Research in Vancouver, Canada, with adults over 60 years old found that 'benches positively contributed to older adults' mobility experiences by: (i) enhancing their use and enjoyment of green and blue spaces; (ii) serving as a mobility aid; and (iii) contributing to social cohesion and social capital' (Ottoni et al., 2016, p. 33). This research found the presence of benches in the community significantly contributes to spaces being accessible for older adults across the mobility spectrum and enhances social capital by facilitating opportunities to interact with others.

Some have speculated whether the current focus on movement and activity has caused an 'inequitable allocation of space and resources for movement over places to stay' (Legge, 2020, p. 441). Whether this notion has merit must be carefully evaluated. But public space needs both affordances for sitting and for being active, and any well-designed space intended specifically for physical activity should always afford opportunities to rest.

Designing better seats

Simply providing seating in urban environments is a good start. But many of the seats we see in public spaces today can be better designed. We need to create seating that is inviting, will contribute to the character and essence of the place, is specific to user needs, is functional and ergonomic, is aesthetically pleasing, is low maintenance, and is affordable to create and install. Not a small list! And not a simple task to be left as the last decision of the design process. Finding the cheapest option in the outdoor furniture catalogue at hand is not likely to lead to a great decision, nor is using the same option over and over again. Unless having a unified, signature look is part of the design intent for a given area, as is the case with the carriage green benches in Paris. Either way, the decision about seating requires thought and consideration.

Ergonomics

Admittedly, most public seating is only meant for temporary or intermittent use by any one person. Benches are designed for people to use for a short time, rather than all day and because of this, comfort may not be the most important design consideration. Ergonomics considers body size and weight, so if the potential users include a broad spectrum of body sizes, it is almost impossible to create a one-size-fits-all option.

According to a Dutch study (Swart et al., 2009), older adults prefer seats that have armrests, a seat height between 45 and 50 cm (17–20 inches), and a seat depth of a maximum of 44.5 cm (17.5 inches). Seat widths for individuals should be between 52 and 60 cm (20–23 inches). A back rest is also important and should be at an angle of 90–110 degrees, relative to the seat, at a maximum height of 35–45 cm (13–17 inches). Older adults in the study also prefer seating to accommodate four to six people to gather in a group. And finally, the research showed that waste bins near seating were a must for older adults (see Chapter 2 for a discussion on trash bins), likely a common desire for all ages.

When designing seats specifically for younger populations, cultural groups, or people with disabilities or mobility needs, dimensions need to be adjusted. In some cases, very basic seating options may be preferred as they are not designed specifically for anyone of a particular physical size or body type and can accommodate a wide range of needs. New ergonomic forms are now possible with 3D printing and advances in fabrication technologies. For example, the benches designed for Harvard Plaza in Cambridge, Massachusetts, by Stoss Landscape Urbanism used parametric modelling to create '17 benches, made up of 7 types, each with similar ergonomically-sound geometries' (Green, 2013). As shown in Figure 3.1, these sculptural wooden benches can be customised to suit different needs, accommodate different bodies and seating positions, enabling people to sit alone or in groups, with options for sun and shade and soft low-energy LED lighting at night.

Scholars have suggested that the way we design public seating may need to change to accommodate an ageing population and a growing number of people with movement or physiological limitations (Kamenikova, 2013). This is a concern that needs to be addressed into the future. The physical and psychological characteristics of the people using a space and the elements within it are a key consideration when designing affordances for sitting. Understanding the needs, limitations, and challenges of the user is a critical component of effective design.

Sitting down 49

Figure 3.1 Benches in Harvard Plaza designed by Stoss Landscape Urbanism.
Credit: Charles Mayer.

Location, location, location … why seating arrangements matter

The placement of seating in public spaces can dictate whether it is used or not. Prospect Refuge Theory tells us that people prefer to sit where they feel protected (refuge), yet also have a view of what is happening around them (prospect) (Cushing & Miller, 2020). This aspect of human nature can be seen when popular seating is placed on the outside edge of public spaces, providing a view inward, or when a seat is placed on top of a hill to provide a view outward. Even before our recognition of this theory, designers understood the importance of effective seating location. In early modern Italy, piazzas were often built with a horseshoe of tiered seating that enabled the public to watch the spectacle within, be it for political, ceremonial, or entertainment purposes (Elet, 2002).

Seating arrangements to socially orchestrate or programme a space is a common practice for events and gatherings. Whether the intent is to get people to socialise in small groups, to pay attention to someone or something on a stage, to sit independently and study or do work, or to accommodate a very large gathering of people in the most efficient way possible, the arrangement of the seating is important. When placement has not been considered carefully, seating can be observed backing onto a busy road, or with no view to speak of. Figure 3.2 shows an example of poorly placed bench that is backing onto a busy urban street. Although seating can be provided purely for convenience in places where a rest stop might be necessary, such as walking up a long hill, or in places where people may need to wait for something like a train or bus, it is still important to place the seating appropriately.

Sometimes, seating is all about the view. Views of green and blue spaces can be calming, and those that provide an extended view can orient people and give them a sense of security. Seating placed strategically can also help accentuate an overlook.

As discussed in *Creating Great Places*, the arrangement of seating is important for personal space and is a focus for proxemics (Cushing & Miller, 2020). British psychiatrist Humphrey Osmond is credited with describing two patterns or arrangements that either promote or limit social interactions – sociopetal and sociofugal (Meagher & Marsh, 2017). Osmond made contributions to the field of socioarchitecture, with his research in mental hospitals informing his thoughts on these spatial arrangements (Sommer, 2004). According to the APA Dictionary of Psychology (https://dictionary.apa.org/), sociopetal describes 'environmental conditions that promote social interaction, such as circular seating arrangements and a comfortable ambient room temperature'. Sociopetal seating faces inward, such as the chairs around a table, to enable conversation and interaction. In contrast, the term sociofugal

Figure 3.2 A bench is poorly placed with its back to a busy road in downtown Brisbane.
Credit: Debra Cushing.

describes environmental conditions that discourage or prevent social interaction, such as rows of seats facing the same way, as with church pews (https://dictionary.apa.org/).

These common seating arrangements influence the activities in a place. Benches arranged in a linear fashion, for example, facilitate looking out in one direction to watch something, such as the benches lining a sports field, or along a street. In contrast, seating arranged in a circular fashion is more conducive to conversations and connecting with other people. Such arrangements can be seen in examples such as Danish Landscape Architect Jens Jensen's council ring[2] or in the commonly referenced 'yarning circle' of First Nations Peoples in Australia which emphasises creating a safe place for all people to have their say without judgement.[3]

According to pre-COVID Research in Hong Kong on urban park seating patterns, park visitors in groups of two preferred linear bench arrangements, while groups of three to five preferred a circular arrangement to enable better interactions and greater eye contact (Luximon et al., 2015). Depending on the specific activities desired in the space, providing a mixture of options will give flexibility to different people and different activities, potentially making a space more versatile.

Providing multiple seating options can address different people's needs and characteristics and make the space more usable and inviting. Seating that can be changed in some way by the user provides practical advantages. William H. Whyte (1980), for example, loved moveable chairs and the flexibility and control they afford people to create the level of intimacy they desired. This works well for when people want to sit closer to each other, such as parents with young children, or when people feel the need to social distance or to create extra space when sitting next to strangers. Moveable seating also gives people the ability to move their seat according to their comfort and preference, into or out of the sun/shade, closer or further from a splashing fountain, or away from a high traffic walkway. Moveable chairs can also be added or subtracted to accommodate different gathering sizes, and to restrict the number of people who can sit in one area which was useful at the height of COVID-19 restrictions.

In contemporary urban spaces, seating can be provided, or not, to determine the uses of public spaces, and the size of the gathering. When the intent is to limit gathering, then fewer seats can be put into an area. Or when the desire is to accommodate a lot of people, many seats or flexible seating is often the solution. In cases where large events do not happen regularly, it may be preferred that seating is brought in to accommodate the influx of people. Moveable seating provides choice and adaptability, and when people can control the seating arrangement, they can adapt the space to their needs and comfort levels.

Benches that make an emotional statement

Seating in public spaces does not always blend in and go unnoticed. In some cases, alternative uses of seating may be considered 'undesirable' because it limits use by a majority of people to accommodate just a few. Activities such as sleeping rough in parks, skate boarding, or even locking a bicycle to the side of a bench can prevent others from using the seat at certain times. In a story posted in the BBC online titled '"Design Crimes" how a bench launched a homelessness debate', Chris Bell (2018) discusses the issue of anti-homeless bars on benches in Calgary, Canada. Highlighting a debate that played out on twitter after a photo of a rainbow painted bench with circular arm rests bisecting the seating area was posted. The debate centred around whether the arm rests were there to prevent homeless people from sleeping on them, or if they actually helped people with limited mobility, such as older people, to stand up from a seated position. While the underlying intention of the bench appears to have been appropriate and equitable, the debate shows the importance of cues for communicating affordances and care.

Seating can also make a statement simply by the paint colour. The Red Bench Project, launched in 2019 in Australia by the Red Rose Foundation, aims to raise awareness about domestic violence in the community.[4] Founded by Betty Taylor, a domestic abuse prevention advocate, the Red Rose Foundation placed red benches in schools, sporting clubs, and other community spaces as a way to start conversations about ending domestic and family violence. The benches include a plaque with the words 'Domestic Violence: Let's Change the Ending' (see Figure 3.3).

A sculpture of seating can also serve as a landmark or photo opportunity, even if it is not actually for sitting. It can be designed as an artistic expression to evoke or provoke an emotional response. An evocative sculpture titled Melancholy, created by Albert Gyorgy in Lake Geneva, Switzerland, represents the hollow, empty feeling when someone you love dies. It shows a slumped hollowed figure sitting with its head down and the weight of the intense pain on its shoulders.[5] See Figure 3.4 for an image of Gyorgy's emotive sculpture.

Similarly, the popular movie provider Netflix has donated benches to communities in the United Kingdom in support of mental health. The show 'After Life', created by comedian Ricky Gervais, features

Figure 3.3 One of the benches from the Red Bench Project, located in Indooroopilly, Queensland, Australia.

Credit: Debra Cushing.

54   **Unremarkable elements**

Figure 3.4 Melancholy by sculpture artist Albert Gyorgy.
Credit: Art_inthecity (Flickr CC).

his character Tony sitting on a park bench after the death of his wife. According to an Internet post (Starkey, 2022), 'The benches were commissioned with suicide prevention charity the Campaign Against Living Miserably (Calm) and feature QR codes leading to online resources and a message of support'. They're also inscribed with a quote from the third season of 'After Life', 'Hope is everything' and can be found in numerous locations around London and other cities.

Seating is also commonly used for memorials. In New York City's Central Park, benches are used as memorials and gifts, with most including a dedication plaque to celebrate and honour a loved one. This Adopt-a-Bench programme was established in 1986 by the Central Park Conservancy and has helped raise significant funds for park maintenance over the years. As of 2022, over 7,000 benches had been dedicated, creating meaningful attachments to the park for many people.[6]

Can we nudge certain actions with the design of seating?

Using seating to nudge specific activities is not a new concept. Again, looking back to fifteenth-century Florence and the grand piazzas outside the palaces of powerful families, we note that seating in certain locations and arrangements was used to control where people gathered and how they experienced the space; 'There must also have been a measure of social control in this process; by shaping the urban fabric, the patron could shape urban experience around his house' (Elet, 2002, p. 459). And just think of the childhood game of musical chairs – when the music stops everyone scrambles for a chair, yet someone is left without one. Providing or not providing a chair for everyone causes the players to respond in certain ways and nudges their behaviour and choices.

Rather than using seating as a form of social control, we can use it to nudge people to stay in public spaces, to bring life to it, socialise, and connect. As a nudge, a bench sends powerful cues that it is okay to stop and rest, to watch what is happening, to simply be, in a space. The following propositions demonstrate how seating can nudge both salutogenic and playable actions.

Proposition 1: Creating salutogenic outdoor spaces with seating that nudge physical movement in a playful way

We most often think of being stationary when sitting. But what if seating could get us moving more? To accommodate the need to be active in public spaces and counteract the implications of physical inactivity, seating can include elements that prompt movement such as bouncing benches or swings. Or flat benches that are placed in convenient locations to provide a space for people who are already active, a chance to do box jumps, push-ups, split lunges, step-ups, dips, stretches, and other movements. Or signs and other cues can be provided to give people ideas for actions and movements.

One example popping up on placemaking blogs is the urban swing. Swing Time, designed by Höweler + Yoon Architecture, is one example of this. The design includes glowing circular swings originally placed as an installation within a temporary park named the Lawn on D between the Boston Convention Centre and Exhibition Centre (Mairs, 2014). The design promotes healthy behaviour, that is also fun and different. The architects were quoted explaining 'We had the idea of a playscape in the city that engages people of all ages in active play' (Mairs, 2014). The LED lights respond to activity, with the white lights indicating the swing is motionless, and the purple light indicating it is in motion. The 20 swings are made of polypropylene and suspended from steel scaffolding.

According to the Massachusetts Convention Centre Authority (MCCA) blog (Wright, 2016), the installation is extremely popular and is now in its third iteration. Changes have included a solar canopy with photovoltaics and batteries installed over the swings to enable them to run on solar power. As shown in Figure 3.5, the revised design also includes a more streamlined and robust swing that takes advantage of new fabrication processes.

Similarly, the Unite/Unire project in Rome, Italy, focuses on 'bodily awareness through direct engagement with an active-design landscape'. The concrete and plywood bench installation was designed by the Urban Movement Design team, and was the winning project of the 2012 Young Architects Program of the Museum of the Twenty-First Century Art (MAXXI).[7] The seating installation was designed purposefully to afford people the opportunity to assume different seated or lying postures, allowing people to stretch and move in different ways, and at three levels of difficulty. Designs like this that encourage movement can help get more people active and are more remarkable.

Proposition 2: Nudging climate change awareness and sustainability with bench design

Can public seating help raise awareness for climate change implications in the hopes of nudging sustainability actions? Potentially.

Acknowledging it is now common to see benches and outdoor furniture made of recycled materials, the reality is that these designs sometimes lack sophistication and interest. Many sustainable seating options use recycled plastic moulded to look like timber, but it clearly isn't. Although some examples are well done, too many are clunky, and lack the detail or textural qualities you would find in similar products made with real wood or metal. We can and must do better. However, when the recycled designs are honest about their materiality to authentically send a message about what they are made of and why, it can contribute to the character and success of the space and be more interesting and engaging – essentially, more remarkable.

One example of this authenticity is the sculptural benches and seating designed by artist Colin Selig (Metcalf, 2013) an American artist from

Sitting down 57

Figure 3.5 Swing Time at the Boston Convention Center.
Credit: John Horner; Courtesy of Höweler + Yoon Architecture.

San Francisco, California. Selig creates climate conscious sculptural pieces from regionally sourced salvage propane tanks, dissected and reassembled. The already curving pieces of metal fit the ergonomic needs of the human body. The first one was built in 2010, and since then he has earned several awards and honours for his designs, including the Exhibiter's Choice Award at the 2012 Smithsonian Craft Show Awards. As seen in Figure 3.6, some of the sculptural pieces have been

58   Unremarkable elements

Figure 3.6 Colin Selig's sculptural benches made from recycled propane tanks.
Credit: Colin Selig; Colin Selig; Suzanne Gray (alligator bench); Colin Selig.

exhibited in locations across the United States.[8] These designs may not nudge direct action, but they may be effective as conversation starters that get people talking and thinking, which is often an important step in taking environmental action.

In Copenhagen, Denmark, as in many other places around the world, sea level rise is a serious concern. Ten benches placed in key locations around the city have been elevated and fitted with a copper plaque, 'Flooding will become part of our everyday life unless we start doing something about our climate. According to the latest UN Climate Report sea-levels are expected to rise up to 1 metre before 2100 if global warming continues' (Brown, 2022; Kakani, 2022). The benches have been raised 85 cm (33 inches) above a normal bench height, commissioned by a Danish TV station, TV2, as part of a climate change awareness campaign called 'Our Earth – our responsibility'. Sea level rise is of serious concern in the city, since it is in a low-lying region, with some areas only a few metres above sea level.[9]

Conclusion

Seating is an important amenity in urban public spaces. Described as the humble and ubiquitous un-sung hero, public seating can be disregarded as an afterthought. If left as an unremarkable element, it could undermine a public space, or make people not want to stay in that space. But if we take the time to think more carefully and purposefully about the design of seating in any space, it has immense potential to change the way a space is used.

This chapter aims to raise the element of public seating to a new level of awareness, and respect for what well-designed and well-placed seating can do. From the Red Bench project to raise awareness for domestic violence, to the playful Swing Time seating in Boston, to the high benches in Copenhagen that raise awareness of expected rising sea levels, the design of seating can nudge salutogenic, playable, and sustainable behaviours. By raising awareness about specific and serious global issues or simply encouraging people to have fun and play, seating can change how we interact, or are impacted by our public spaces. They can be more remarkable.

Notes

1 See https://www.uclahealth.org/spinecenter/ergonomics-prolonged-sitting#
   :~:text=Sitting%20for%20prolonged%20periods%20of,back%20
   muscles%20and%20spinal%20discs
2 See https://www.gcamerica.org/news/get/id/2640
3 See https://www.qcaa.qld.edu.au/about/k-12-policies/aboriginal-torres-strait-
   islander-perspectives/resources/yarning-circles#:~:text=A%20yarning%20
   circle%20is%20a,be%20heard%20and%20to%20respond

4 See https://www.lgaq.asn.au/news/article/1166/the-red-bench-project-changing-the-ending-to-domestic-violence and https://www.redrose foundation.com.au/red-bench-project
5 See https://www.penwellgabeltopeka.com/Blog/6245/Melancoliesculpture
6 See https://www.centralparknyc.org/giving/adopt-a-bench
7 See https://michaelcaton.com/Unite-Unire-1
8 The benches are on display on the artist website at https://www.colinselig.com.
9 For a story about the raised benches in Denmark, see https://youtu.be/0UoMhIorZZI.

References

Bell, C. (2018). *'Design Crimes' how a bench launched a homelessness debate.* Downloaded 29 July 2022 from https://www.bbc.com/news/blogs-trending-44107320

Brown, H. (May 11, 2022). Copenhagen's unusually high benches are raising the alarm on climate change. *Euronews.green.* Downloaded 30 July 2022 from https://www.euronews.com/green/2022/05/10/copenhagen-s-weirdly-tall-benches-are-a-warning-about-climate-change

Charleton, A. (2022). *Why are all Paris benches, signs and fences green?* Downloaded from https://www.afrenchcollection.com/why-paris-benches-signs-and-fences-are-green/

Cushing, & Miller (2020). *Creating great places: Evidence-based urban design for health and well-being.* Routledge.

Elet, Y. (2002). Seats of power: The outdoor benches of early modern Florence. *Journal of the Society of Architectural Historians*, 61(4), 444–469.

Green, J. (2013). The humble public bench becomes comfortable, inclusive, and healthy. *The Dirt.* Downloaded from https://dirt.asla.org/2013/12/18/the-humble-public-bench-becomes-comfortable-inclusive-and-healthy/

Guernier, P. (n.d.) *What is the story behind the public benches of Paris?* Downloaded from https://frenchmoments.eu/benches-of-paris/

Kakani, K. (June 17, 2022). The alarming reason Denmark's Copenhagen has elevated its public benches. *Timesnow.com.* Downloaded 30 July 2022 from https://www.timesnownews.com/viral/the-alarming-reason-denmarks-copenhagen-has-elevated-its-public-benches-article-92279973

Kamenikova, V. (2013). Seating furniture for public interior (creating of non-discriminatory interior for people with limitations and seniors). *Acta Universitatis Agriculturae et Silviculturae Mendelianae Brunensis*, *LXI*, 1725–1731.

Lee, J. (2021). *The park bench is an endangered species.* Downloaded from https://www.nytimes.com/2021/10/12/magazine/park-benches.html

Legge, K. (2020). Public seating: Small important places. In C. Courage, T. Borrup, M.R. Jackson, K. Legge, A. McKeown, L. Platt, & J. Schupbach (Eds.), *The Routledge handbook of placemaking* (1st ed., pp. 439–448). Routledge. https://doi.org/10.4324/9780429270482.

Luximon, Y., Kwong, H. Y., & Tai, Y. Y. (2015). User preferences of urban park seating pattern in Hong Kong. *Procedia Manufacturing*, 3, 4273–4278. https://doi.org/10.1016/j.promfg.2015.07.415

Mairs, J. (2014). Höweler + Yoon Architecture installs a glow-in-the-dark swing set in Boston. *Dezeen.com.* Downloaded 30 July 2022 from https://www.dezeen.com/2014/09/25/howeler-yoon-architecture-swing-time-playground-boston-glow-in-the-dark/

Meagher, B., & Marsh, K. (2017). Seeking the safety of sociofugal space: Environmental design preferences following social ostracism. *Journal of Experimental Social Psychology*, 68, 192–199.

Metcalf, J. (2013). Sustainable, stylish furniture made from cut-up propane tanks. *Bloomberg Asia Edition*. Downloaded 1 August 2022 from https://www.bloomberg.com/news/articles/2013-05-31/sustainable-stylish-furniture-made-from-cut-up-propane-tanks

Ottoni, C., Sims-Gould, J., Winters, M., Heijnen, M., & McKay, H. (2016). 'Benches become like porches': Built and social environment influences on older adults' experiences of mobility and well-being. *Social Science & Medicine*, 169, 33–41.

PPS.org. (n.d.). *What makes a successful space?* Downloaded 22 July 2022 from https://www.pps.org/article/grplacefeat

Sommer, R. (2004). In memoriam: Humphry Osmond. *Journal of Environmental Psychology*, 24(2004), 257–258.

Starkey, A. (2022). Netflix donates benches to local councils in 'After Life' mental health scheme. *NME.com* (18th January 2022). Downloaded 30 July 2022 from https://www.nme.com/en_au/news/tv/netflix-donates-benches-councils-after-life-mental-health-scheme-3140962

Stoppard, L. (2020) – How the Park Bench became the unlikely epicentre of the nation's social life, British VOGUE online. 17 November 2022. Downloaded 22 July 2022 from https://www.vogue.co.uk/arts-and-lifestyle/article/park-benches

Swart, T., Molenbroek, J., Langveld, L., van Brederode, M., & Daams, B. (2009, Fall). Outdoor seating design to facilitate social interaction among older adults. *Ergonomics in Design*, 17(4), 4–27.

Vallance, J., Gardiner, P., Lynch, B., D'Silva, A., Boyle, T., Taylor, L., Johnson, S., Buman, M., & Owen, N. (2018). Evaluating the evidence on sitting, smoking, and health: Is sitting really the new smoking? *American Journal of Public Health*, 108(11), 1478. https://doi.org/10.2105/AJPH.2018.304649

Whyte, W. (1980). *The social life of small urban spaces*. Project for Public Spaces.

Wright, N. (2016). *Swing Time 3.0 Debuts at the Lawn on D Powered by Citizen's Bank*. Downloaded 30 July 2020 from https://blog.signatureboston.com/swing-time-3.0-debuts-at-the-lawn-on-d-powered-by-citizens-bank

4 Moving up

Redesigning stairs to be more remarkable

There is something fascinating and mysterious about seeing a staircase and wondering what is at the top. In the same way that walking along a trail and being drawn to whatever is around a corner or through a gate, our preference for different landscapes is often related to a sense of mystery and a search for information (Kaplan et al., 1989). In addition to the concept of mystery, stairs are often used as a visual metaphor in movies to represent an obstacle ahead, achieving a goal, obtaining power and becoming enlightened. If you think of the connotations and symbolism around climbing a ladder and moving up, it often represents progress, being future focused, and attaining a better position or status. Staircases and steps are used to refer to different phases of a process, again often referring to the top point as the culmination or ultimate destination.

Stairs are also common in our everyday environments and can be part of our daily routines. In a purposeful attempt to increase my incidental physical activity and achieve the target of 10,000 steps per day, I have committed to always taking the stairs when the journey is under five stories. That has been an adventurous choice and, too often, not a successful or enjoyable one. The internal stairwells of large hotels, commercial office buildings, and university buildings are typically accessed via unloved fire exit stairs: once found, the stairwells themselves are bland, dark, narrow, sometimes dirty, slightly damp, and very hard to locate and use, with the fire doors heavy to open and frequently locked or accessible only via a staff/resident access card. Many times, I have reached my third or fourth floor destination, and been unable to enter with the fire exit doors locked from the inside, meaning I must traipse back down the stairs to use the elevators.

The use of stairs is often discouraged in buildings that were built after elevators became common or in buildings above a certain height. The elevator is often visually dominant and centrally located as the main way to ascend to upper floors. In public spaces, stairs are sometimes avoided if the topography can be modified or if ramps can be

DOI: 10.4324/9781003052746-5

added for universal accessibility. But it is not the presence of stairs that we need to rethink, it is how they are designed and where they are located. In a world where an estimated 60%–80% of our population is obese or overweight, designing out opportunities for incidental physical activity and movement – such as taking the stairs – is a missed opportunity.

Designers must also recognise that our experience with stairs is not always positive. Stairs can be dangerous, causing people to trip and lose their footing. Falling down the stairs is a common fear for older adults and young children who are not as agile or are developing their motor skills and coordination. Research suggests that people carrying large bags, women, obese people, older adults, and people with mobility limitations are more likely than other groups to avoid taking the stairs (Eves, 2014; Gay et al., 2022). Impairments, both temporary and long term, can sometimes be seen as insurmountable barriers to getting someplace via stairs. Stairs can also be daunting. The non-descript fire-safe grey stairwell has been the site of countless close calls or fatal attacks in movies and crime shows for understandable reasons. The spaces are often dark, malodorous, and intimidating, misaligned with CPTED (Crime Prevention Through Environmental Design) principles.

Sadly, staircases can also be the site for anti-social behaviour and suicides. Take, for example, the spiral staircase sculpture known as the 'Vessel' in the Hudson Yards Public Square in Manhattan, New York, which opened in 2019. Imagined by Thomas Heatherwick and Heatherwick Studio as an interactive artwork 150 feet high, the Vessel features 154 interconnecting flights of stairs nearly 2,500 individual steps and 80 landings. The vertical climb offers remarkable views of the city and the Hudson River from different heights, angles, and vantage points. The sculpture became a popular site for Instagram photos and was even the backdrop for a music video by the Chainsmokers for their pop song, 'Takeaway'. Tragically, it has since become the site of four suicides, and just two years after opening, it closed indefinitely. Discussions are ongoing about making the structure safer and more usable, and it is an important reminder that design and material choice for any staircase requires significant thought and consideration.

This chapter focuses very specifically on how we might positively redesign unremarkable experiences of moving up in buildings and public open spaces. We look at how we might capitalise on the positive aspects of stairs and the experience of moving up, or down, to create staircases that are salutogenic, sustainable, and playable. Stairs can play a large role in our physical environment and in our daily experiences, so getting their design right is critical.

From mechanics to memorable: the evolution of staircase design

As an important architectural feature of buildings and public spaces, it is important to look at how staircases have evolved. Common staircase configurations have been used throughout history, often going in and out of favour, including those that are straight, cantilevered, spiral, and dog legged. We only touch on their history here, but other scholars have covered it extensively, highlighting their evolution, their construction, and their meaning (see, e.g., Campbell & Tutton, 2014).

Moving up and down has always been a necessity for humans, with steps carved into rock faces or created using large blocks of stone. Early pyramids or ziggurats in Mesoamerica and Mesopotamia, were constructed with stepped faces that people ascended for ceremonial or religious purposes (Campbell & Tutton, 2014). Stairs were given symbolic or strategic meaning, either used for defence purposes, or to demonstrate a hierarchy in society. Grand exterior staircases demarking the entrance to important government buildings or palaces were used to show importance, grandeur, and power. The act of climbing to a destination means it requires effort and therefore puts emphasis and value on what is at the top.

Stairs were a necessity until the invention of the elevator and the safety break in the 1850s by Elisha G. Otis (Nichols, 2018), although crude versions using hoists and pullies were around much earlier. The adoption of the elevator in buildings enabled additional floors to be added and changed the way vertical movement happened. Gradually, stairs in multi-story buildings became less about aesthetics and symbolism and more about function, safety, and efficiency. This was translated into stairways being regulated to the corners of buildings, often with a basic neon exit sign above.

Coming full circle, many large contemporary buildings and urban sites today increasingly treat the stairs as a centrepiece that surprises and connects, as seen in Figure 4.1. From cantilevered or 'floating', to transparent and spiral, to large impactful staircases in the centre of building entrances, to terraced seating integrated into indoor and outdoor staircases, the contemporary form and structure of stairs is once again central, symbolic, innovative, and celebrated. In contemporary spaces, stairs can and should take centre stage, with the elevator less visually accessible.

Why climb the stairs? Physical and mental health benefits of stair climbing

At the outset, it is important to emphasise the physical health benefits of choosing to take the stairs. At first glance, taking the stairs might

Moving up 65

Figure 4.1 External stairs at Darling Harbor, Sydney, Australia.
Credit: Evonne Miller.

appear to involve relatively minimal levels of physical activity. But in fact, going up the stairs is a vigorous-intensity activity, and going down the stairs is moderate intensity (Gay et al., 2022). The US National Physical Activity Guidelines (2018) encourage shorter bouts of walking up and down stairs to contribute to physical health. Research shows that brief, vigorous stair climbing is effective in increasing cardio-respiratory fitness within cardiac rehabilitation exercise programmes

(Dunford et al., 2021), and that daily stair climbing may be protective against metabolic syndrome (Whittaker et al., 2021). Climbing stairs can also provide more energy that a shot of caffeine! Studying active, but sleep deprived, young women, Randolph and O'Connor (2017) found that compared to a low dose (50 mg) of caffeine, 10 minutes of low-to-moderate intensity stair walking increased feelings of energy.

Stair climbing can be seen as an intentional form of exercise, think of the vertical climbing machines you see at the gym or a Stadium Stomp event at a major sports stadium. But it can also be categorised as a NEAT activity. NEAT stands for Non-exercise Activity Thermogenesis and represents the incidental physical movements we do throughout the day. NEAT and incidental physical activity, such as walking, climbing, standing, and fidgeting (Levine, 2002), are fundamental components of energy expenditure. NEAT is likely to contribute between 15% and 50% of total daily energy expenditure, depending on individual characteristics (Levine et al., 2006).

Stair climbing may also be good for your mental health, but there is a lack of research on its impacts and psychological benefits (Gay et al., 2022). If we can use stairs to create opportunities for socially connecting with others, there may be additional connections between stair climbing and mental health, since research suggests that socialising and interacting with others is good for us (Bath & Deeg, 2005). Staircases, for example, can be a social hub in contemporary workplaces, connecting people from different divisions and departments, and providing a site for communal gatherings and unexpected social connections and interactions. Terraced staircases provide unique and flexible areas for meeting and co-working, encouraging chance meetings and increasingly serving as the visual and social focal point of contemporary designs, as we saw in Figure 4.1.

And while many of our examples include internal staircases in workplaces or public buildings, there are also examples from across the globe of staircases transforming and activating urban spaces. In Hong Kong, the Edge Design Institute has converted an ordinary public stairway into a socially engaging public area called The Cascade Project. Featuring individual and adjoining seating, this asymmetric mesh sculpture is surrounded by plants and is strategically lit at night, turning an unremarkable concrete staircase in The Centrium into a safe, inviting, and sociable space, as the inspiring images in Figure 4.2 illustrate. In higher density Hong Kong, where space is at a premium, this repurposed staircase has transformed an underutilised public thoroughfare into a socially active public space. By thinking 'outside the box', and not accepting the rules as written, The Cascade Project is a powerful exemplar of the creative conversion of stairs into a community space.

Moving up 67

Figure 4.2 The Cascade Project in Hong Kong.
Credit: Images courtesy of Edge Design Institute.

Designing stairs and escalators

The primary function of staircases is to provide inter-level access, notably there are minimum standards to guide designers. In Australia, for example, staircases must slope at an angle of 20° to 45°, with a recommended angle of between 30° and 38°. All stairs must have uniform dimensions within a maximum of ±5 mm and the treads must be slip resistant, visible and extend across the full width of the stairway. A single flight can use a maximum of 18 stairs or risers, connected by landings (Worksafe QLD, 2020). The creative and innovative use of materials, combined with strategic and thoughtful placement, as well as design imagination, can transform the daily activity of 'taking the stairs' into an experience.

You can well appreciate that how a stairway is designed will impact how people perceive and use it, and sometimes whether or not they can even find it. A study by Nicoll (2007) suggests that spatial qualities optimising convenience and the ability to find the stairs may have the most influence on stair use in buildings. The study evaluated stair use in 10 university buildings and determined that three key variables explained 53% of stair use: the effective area of each step; the extent to which a stair is visible from other interior spaces within a building; and the number of turns for travel from the most integrated path.

The location is also a key consideration. The central location of the dramatic Helix staircase at the Experimentarium Science Centre in Copenhagen, Denmark, is one such example. Built from steel cladding with 10 tons of copper, the form of this large, bold staircase was inspired by the structure of DNA. The prominent location also means you cannot miss this staircase upon arrival at the building, and people are more likely to want to use these visually dramatic stairs.

Location is also a key defining feature of the escalator at the famous Centre Pompidou in central Paris, constructed in 1977 by Richard Rogers and Renzo Piano (see Figure 4.3). Running up the external facade of this iconic, radical, highly flexible, and multi-colour modern museum is a giant six-story diagonal escalator, sometimes referred to as a moving staircase, with viewing platforms facing the public square. As a public space, the escalators 'float' across the street, enabling people to see and meet people. Escalators can also reflect their locale, as we see at the Sydney Airport in Australia where this internal escalator is playfully covered by the shape of an airplane.

Because of their configuration, staircases can also be a prime location for interesting messages and artwork. Figure 4.3 illustrates how

Figure 4.3 The black and white spiral staircase of Oodi Helsinki Central Library.
Credit: Nanaro Flickr (CC by 2.0).

the thoughtful design of staircases can welcome people. Designed by ALA Architects, the dramatic black and white spiral stairs of the Oodi Helsinki Central Library links together three stories. On their black exterior are words written in white, provided by community members during the design process. These words describe the type of people welcome in this library, some of which, translated into English, are below and can now also be read online, as a digital experience, in multiple languages.[1]

everyone
strangers
lazybones
the henpecked
the spiritually enlightened
orphans
introverts
fierce fighters
reading clubs
anarchists
officials
sports fans
chubby folk
the lonely
old people
families
victims of war
aspiring authors
the voiceless
the disappointed
babies
humorists
battlers
victims of school bullies
heroes
builders
reformers
zany people
the invisible
presidents
the homeless
singles

Unremarkable elements

schoolchildren
daydreamers
princes
outsiders
winners
the guilty
the pure-hearted
bureaucrats
extraterrestrials
revolutionaries
fault-finders
the depressed
dreamers
authors
grandchildren
agnostics
the silenced
short people
nature lovers
quiet souls
asylum-seekers
hedonists
self-sacrificers
mystics
prudes
the disabled
tourists
sound minds
hippies
citizens
the forsaken
collectors
the landless
dog lovers
lovers
addicts
doers
soldiers
the unknown
cat people
sign language users

witches
vegans
critics
loafers
the masses
the illiterate
heterosexuals
conservatives
LGBT families
scholars
friends
the forgotten
the cheerful
the young
minorities
freeloaders
alcoholics
the hounded
adopted people
small people
curmudgeons
characters
LGBT teens
gigglers
artists
leaders
bored people
challengers
the helpless
busy people
dementia sufferers
the anxious
the brave
phonies
the hopeful
enemies
the misguided
the childless
royals
charlatans
you

Nudging health and sustainability … the propositions

The experience of climbing the stairs can and should be remarkable. The following section includes two propositions that promote spaces that are sustainable and salutogenic. One is about nudging stair climbing as a form of physical activity to improve health. The other is about using environmentally friendly materials to nudge sustainability. As you read these propositions, think about how these nudges could work in different contexts.

Proposition 1: Nudging health by designing salutogenic stairs

There are significant health benefits of climbing the stairs. Short bouts of moderate to vigorous physical activity, like stair climbing, are good for most people. And in many cases, it is a functional form of exercise since it also gets you somewhere. So the question becomes, how can we encourage people to do it more often?

Nudge theory would suggest placing a nudge at the point of choice – the point at which people make the decision to take the stairs or use an elevator or escalator. Research by Lewis and Eves (2012) found that it was more effective to use a volitional nudge then a motivational nudge. This means that a motivational sign inside the elevator was less effective than a point-of-choice prompt positioned at the time and place where people choose the stairs or elevator. Visibility of a prompt at the time when someone makes a behavioural choice is necessary to change actual behaviour.

Multiple nudges can also be used together to reinforce healthy behaviours in one setting. For example, the design of affordable housing in New York included several nudges to promote healthy living and encourage physical activity (Garland et al., 2018). Specifically, the building had central, wide, and well-lit stairwells, with music playing, visible artwork and point-of-decision prompts encouraging their use. Elevators were in a non-prominent location, with a delayed speed, and the building also featured an indoor gym and outdoor exercise circuit. As a result, the residents reported a significant increase in stair use and a decline in body mass index, compared to a control group living in a similar building. Constructed by the same developers, the two affordable housing buildings had nearly identical unit layouts, but the one with health promoting nudges earned a LEED Innovation in Design (ID) Credit for 'Design for Health through Increased Physical Activity'.

A growing body of literature has focused on nudging incidental physical activity through encouraging stair use, typically changing behavioural norms and choices via posters, signs, footprint outlines,

Moving up   73

Figure 4.4 Stairs and elevator decals.
Credit: Elevator decals in Singapore, Evonne Miller.

and decals on stairs themselves, as seen in Figure 4.4 These catchy slogans remind and nudge people to take the stairs rather than the elevator, tapping into people's desire to be healthier, improve heart health, save time, and reduce their carbon footprint by behaving in more environmentally friendly ways such as, 'Push yourself not the button', 'Burn calories, not electricity'.[2]

One of the main barriers to taking the stairs is the perception that it simply takes too long, and that taking the elevator is quicker. However, several workplace studies suggest the opposite, that taking the stairs is often faster especially during peak times! Shah et al. (2011) measured the time it took for four staff in a 6-story busy urban hospital to take the stairs versus the elevator. Taking the stairs was quicker, saving 15 minutes each workday. It took 13.1 seconds to take the stairs between each floor, compared to 35.6 seconds to travel in one of the two elevators, primarily because of the time waiting for the elevator's arrival (usually 1–2 minutes). Staff took 14 trips, ascending and descending. Taking the stairs took 10.3 minutes, compared to 24.6 or 19.6 minutes for taking the outpatient or x-ray elevators. The longest trip by stairs was going six floors in 58 and 92 seconds, and on busy weekday mornings (7–9 am), travelling six floors via elevator took between 1.1 and 6.9 minutes. Taking the stairs resulted in 3% savings per workday, which could translate into both increased fitness and improved productivity.

While the sample size of the above study was small, a vast amount of literature has identified the value of stair climbing as daily, incidental and relatively easy exercise. The barriers to entry for stair climbing are low, with no cost, special skills or equipment required, making stair climbing a plausible health behaviour for most people. For example, a hospital wide 12-week promotional campaign for stair use at the 12-story University Hospital of Geneva, Switzerland resulted in significant behaviour change. The number of one-story staircase ascents or descents increased from 4 to 21 per day, approximately 10 minutes of daily exercise integrated into work time, calculated as 52 kcal per day. This resulted in improved cardiovascular fitness, a loss of 550 g of body weight, and a 1.5 cm decrease of waist circumference (Meyer et al., 2010). These health benefits were the consequence of a quite simple educational intervention; messages on posters, floor stickers at the point-of-choice between stairs and elevators, with the 77 study participants also wearing badges indicating they were doing a stair walking health intervention. Participants were assessed at baseline, 12 weeks, and 6 months, that is 3 months post intervention. Baseline stair climbing was 4.5, reaching a peak of 20.6 during the intervention and dropping to 7.2 in part, the authors noted, due to the unplanned closure of the main central staircase for renovation just after the 12-week intervention. Encouraging people to take stairs at work is a relatively simple technique to foster incidental movement.

While some of the nudge examples described are about programming and encouraging stair climbing as an activity, increasing stair use also requires good design. The stairs need to be visible and accessible, and they need to be wide enough and comfortable enough for many people to use them. In some cases, mediocre design can be modified with messaging and simple interventions like painting the stairwell door a welcoming colour. In other cases, more drastic design interventions need to occur to make the stairwells safe and easily found.

Proposition 2: Nudging sustainability by designing eco-friendly stairs

Building up, rather than out, can be sustainable as it often means a more efficient use of space and resources, a design strategy important in urbanising areas that having growing populations, but little space. It can be better to efficiently use existing infrastructure to build up, instead of investing in greenfield development and encouraging suburban sprawl. To build up, we need access, which means stairs or elevators.

The design of stairs, specifically what they are constructed from, can also contribute to planetary health. While stairs have traditionally been constructed from hardwood or steel, a number of high-profile sites are turning to bamboo. Although not appropriate for all climates or projects, bamboo is a fast growing, renewable grass, which requires few pesticides or herbicides. Bamboo also grows faster than trees, and depending on the variety, can grow at a rate of 3 feet (90 cm) per day and reach full maturity within 1–5 years. And unlike timber, most bamboo can be harvested a few years after planting and then yearly after that, with a sustainable harvesting process keeping the bamboo forest healthy and its root system unharmed, ready to produce more shoots. In comparison to an equivalent tree mass, bamboo absorbs carbon dioxide and releases 35% more oxygen into the atmosphere (see Manandhar et al., 2019; Zea Escamilla et al., 2018).

As well as being a sustainable building material, bamboo can also be a socially responsible choice. Growing naturally in tropical, sub-tropical, and mild temperate regions of Africa, Asia, America, and Oceania, engaging local communities in sustainable bamboo cultivation and manufacturing offers an alternative income source, which also builds on the traditional construction knowledge and skills of local communities who have used bamboo in construction for centuries (Manandhar et al., 2019). Adopting regenerative bamboo-based construction systems, therefore, has the potential to improve 'economies, environments, and livelihoods' (Zea Escamilla et al., 2018, p. 1).

Stairs, both interior and exterior, can be constructed from bamboo. In the Netherlands, large bamboo terraces and stairs – 1,600 m^2 of bamboo decking boards and 2,500 m of bamboo outdoor beams – means people walk on sustainable bamboo stairs to enter Brightlands Chemelot Campus, a smart material, innovation and sustainable manufacturing hub. Also in the Netherlands, the headquarters of innovative stair designers EeStairs have created their internal stairs from FSC-certified wood and bamboo, with solar panels on the roof providing electricity for the space, shaped in the style of their logo.

Although bamboo can be a sustainable solution, in places where it does not grow naturally, it can require significant transport costs and resources. Some species can also become invasive if grown unregulated. It is always important therefore to look at sustainable solutions wholistically, considering multiple factors. In colder climates too, bamboo may not contribute to the sense of place or genius loci of that environment. You can read more about the theory of sense of place in our first book, *Creating Great Places* (Cushing & Miller, 2020).

Conclusion – redesigning stairs to be more remarkable

Beyond the simple function of providing inter-level access, this chapter has illustrated how the thoughtful design of stairs can have a significant and positive impact on human and planetary health and well-being. Stairs can be designed to be more sustainable in how they are manufactured and constructed and purposefully designed to be sustainable. They can also help encourage movement and physical activity to contribute to a salutogenic environment. Since many buildings and public spaces have stairs, there are endless possibilities to redesign these elements to be more remarkable.

Notes

1 See https://www.oodihelsinki.fi/omistuskirjoitus/?omistuskirjoitus_lang=en
2 See https://www.csuohio.edu/sustainability/take-stairs

References

Bath, P. A., & Deeg, D. (2005). Social engagement and health outcomes among older people: Introduction to a special section. *European Journal of Ageing*, 2(1), 24–30. https://doi.org/10.1007/s10433-005-0019-4

Campbell, W., & Tutton, M. (Eds.). (2014). *Staircases: History, repair and conservation*. Routledge.

Cushing, D. & Miller, E. (2020). Creating Great Places: Evidence-based Urban Design for Health and Wellbeing. Routledge.

Dunford, E. C., Valentino, S. E., Dubberley, J., Oikawa, S. Y., McGlory, C., Lonn, E., Jung, M. E., Gibala, M. J., Phillips, S. M., & MacDonald, M. J. (2021). Brief vigorous stair climbing effectively improves cardiorespiratory fitness in patients with coronary artery disease: A randomized trial. *Front Sports Act Living*, 3, 1–12.

Eves, F. F. (2014). Is there any Proffitt in stair climbing? A headcount of studies testing for demographic differences in choice of stairs. *Psychonomic Bulletin & Review*, 21, 71–77.

Garland, E., Garland, V., Peters, D., Doucette, J., Thanik, E., Rajupet, S., & Sanchez, S. H. (2018). Active design in affordable housing: A public health nudge. *Preventive Medicine Reports*, 10, 9–14.

Gay, J. L., Cherof, S. A., LaFlamme, C. C., & O'Connor, P. J. (2022). Psychological aspects of stair use: A systematic review. *American Journal of Lifestyle Medicine*, 16(1), 109–121. https://doi.org/10.1177/1559827619870104

Kaplan, R., Kaplan, S., & Brown, T. (1989). Environmental preference: A comparison of four domains of predictors. *Environment and Behavior*, 21(5), 509–530. https://doi.org/10.1177/0013916589215001

Levine, J. A. (2002). Non-exercise activity thermogenesis (NEAT). *Best Practice & Research: Clinical Endocrinology & Metabolism*, 16(4), 679–702.

Levine, J., Vander Weg, M., & Klesges, R. (2006). Increasing non-exercise activity thermogenesis: A NEAT way to increase energy expenditure in your patients. *Obesity Management*, 2(4), 146–151.

Lewis, A. & Eves, F. (2012). Prompts before the choice is made: Effects of a stair climbing intervention in university buildings. *British Journal of Health Psychology*, 17(3), 631–643.

Manandhar, R., Kim, J., & Kim, J. (2019). Environmental, social and economic sustainability of bamboo and bamboo-based construction materials in buildings. *Journal of Asian Architecture and Building Engineering*, 18(2), 49–59. https://doi.org/10.1080/13467581.2019.1595629

Meyer, P., Kayser, B., Kossovsky, M., Sigaud, P., Carballo, D., Keller, P., Martin, E., Farpour-Lambert, N., Pichard, C., & Mach, F. (2010). Stairs instead of elevators at workplace: Cardioprotective effects of a pragmatic intervention. *European Journal of Cardiovascular Prevention and Rehabilitation*, 17(5), 569–575. https://doi.org/10.1097/HJR.0b013e328338a4dd

Nichols, S. (2018). The evolution of elevators: physical-human interface, digital interaction, and megatall buildings. In *National Academy of Engineering. Frontiers of engineering: Reports on leading-edge engineering from the 2017 symposium*. National Academies Press (US). Retrieved 22 January 2018 from https://www.ncbi.nlm.nih.gov/books/NBK481624/

Nicoll, G. (2007). Spatial measures associated with stair use. *American Journal of Health Promotion*, 21(4s), 346–52.

Physical Activity Guidelines Advisory Committee. (2018). *Physical activity guidelines advisory committee scientific report*. US Department of Health and Human Services.

Randolph, D., & O'Connor, P. (2017). Stair walking is more energizing than low dose caffeine in sleep deprived young women. *Physiology & Behavior*, 174, 128–135. https://doi.org/10.1016/j.physbeh.2017.03.013

Shah, S., O'Byrne, M., Wilson, M., & Wilson, T. (2011). Elevators or stairs? *Canadian Medical Association Journal*, *183*(18), E1353–E1355. https://doi.org/10.1503/cmaj.110961

Whittaker, A. C., Eves, F. F., Carroll, D., Roseboom, T. J., Ginty, A. T., Painter, R. C., & de Rooij, S. R. (2021). Daily stair climbing is associated with decreased risk for the metabolic syndrome. *BMC Public Health*, *21*, 923. https://doi.org/10.1186/s12889-021-10965-9

Worksafe QLD. (2020). *Safe design and use of stairs*. Downloaded 13 September 2022 from https://www.worksafe.qld.gov.au/safety-and-prevention/hazards/workplace-hazards/slips-trips-and-falls/safe-design-and-use-of-stairs

Zea Escamilla, E., Habert, G., Correal Daza, J. F., Archilla, H. F., Echeverry Fernández, J. S., & Trujillo, D. (2018. Industrial or traditional Bamboo construction? *Comparative Life Cycle Assessment (LCA) of Bamboo-Based Buildings. Sustainability*, *10*, 3096.

5 Blocking out

Redesigning walls and fences to be more remarkable

Despite the democratic notion of open space and barrier-free environments, there can be valuable and legitimate reasons for putting up walls and fences. They keep people in and keep people out. They delineate property lines or boundaries. They hide unsightly views and protect people from accessing potentially dangerous land uses, such as industrial yards, construction sites, open mines, and highways. Retaining walls can keep soil and plants in place, and thick reinforced walls can be used as dams to restrict the flow of water, often creating reservoirs for multiple uses. Fences and walls can be used to protect what's inside, in cases like a vegetable garden, cattle yard, dog park, or childcare centre. And they can control the flow of people, animals, or traffic, as highlighted by the famous line from the Robert Frost poem *Mending Walls*, 'Good fences make good neighbors' which refers to keeping livestock from wandering off and causing damage to neighbouring properties.

Fences and walls can be liberating, providing a sense of security and freedom that comes with being protected from intrusions (Davis & Williams, 2008). This security can be both actual and perceived. In the case of celebrities or political figures, it may be necessary to protect the people inside from curious fans or potentially dangerous stalkers. When security measures fail, and walls are breeched, it can be dangerous.

Walls and fences can also have negative connotations. The sense of security offered by a wall or fence, can be one-sided. Research in Poland suggests that fenced parks which are closed at night offer a sense of safety, but also a perceived elitism (Biernacka et al., 2020). They often separate 'us' from 'them', or the 'haves' from the 'have-nots'. The concept of the gated community is a prime example. A symbol of wealth and status, they can also represent disconnection and isolation. And they send a clear message that only certain people can enter through the gate. Similarly, neighbours who suddenly erect a high stockade fence around their property, blocking a view for others,

DOI: 10.4324/9781003052746-6

or the local government that installs a barrier to prevent people from accessing land that was previously open for use, communicate that only certain people are allowed. As Davis and Williams (2008) wrote 'The damnation of fences and walls highlights the inconvenience and insult implicit in fences and critiques the complex of motivations that informs the erection of barriers' (p. 246).

Some walls also represent political and cultural divisions. The wall between the southern border of the United States and Mexico to control illegal smuggling was hotly debated and contested, for example. Historically significant walls have become cultural icons or landmarks, such as the Great Wall of China, Hadrian's Wall in England, and the Berlin Wall in Germany. And Americans of a certain age may remember President Ronald Regan's iconic line in his 1987 speech at the Brandenburg Gate in Berlin, 'Mr Gorbechev, tear down this wall' (Robinson, 2007). The memorable speech came two years before the wall came down, which symbolised the fall of the Iron Curtain and the fall of communism in Eastern and Central Europe.

Although often seen as micro-elements, walls and fences can have incredible power and impact on how we view and experience our spaces. Research has highlighted the ubiquitous nature of fencing, and the fact that it receives far less attention than roads, powerlines, and other types of linear infrastructure (Jakes et al., 2018). And unlike roads and other infrastructure, fences are typically unregulated and are erected largely by private landowners. Estimates based on spatial data from southern Alberta, Canada show that the linear extent of fences was twice that of all roads per township (Ibid). Yet, these elements that facilitate 'blocking out' have incredible potential to contribute to our experiences in the urban environment, both positively and negatively.

This chapter will highlight several unique and well-designed examples of walls and fences from across the globe. We discuss how these types of common urban elements are much more valuable when designed with an eye to sustainability, playability, and salutogenic design. Walls planted with vegetation as green walls or vertical gardens, walls designed as climbing walls to encourage active play and physical activity, and walls that are painted with art murals as a form of cultural expression, can send positive cues to care. Fences that are designed for safety and protection, but with careful consideration and awareness of exclusionary impacts and perceptions, can improve places rather than cause additional social or environmental issues.

Designing walls and fences for different uses

Although the purpose and function are critical for how walls and fences are perceived, their materiality and aesthetic value are equally important. There is a wealth of technical knowledge that covers walls and fences, including their design for load bearing, thermal mass, and material stability. And we acknowledge that the act of blocking out can be done with many different materials and designs according to their use and purpose. In this section, we discuss their design in regard to creating spaces that are inviting, pleasant, functional, and also beautiful or interesting.

They can be permeable or impermeable, transparent, semi-transparent, or completely solid. They can be made of stone, brick, mud, aluminium, barbed wire, chain-link, timber, glass, or nearly anything. They can be hedgerows planted with living shrubs or trees planted in a line to create a barrier, or solid brick and mortar walls that have a solid earthy quality. Today it is also common to have virtual fences that you cannot see but you can feel. For example, many dog owners have invisible fences around their property that will give their pet a small shock if it goes across the fence line. Often using a system of underground cables, and electric currents transmitted to a special collar worn around the dog's neck. But to others, there is no visible fence present that alters how the space is used or perceived.

Height, thickness, and location matter. Walls and fences represent a vertical plane within a space and their characteristics will impact their actual and perceived effectiveness. A functional fence that is intended to keep animals out, for example, must be high enough to prevent them from jumping over, or low enough to prevent them from climbing under. But a wall that more symbolically demarks a property boundary, can be shorter, even serving as a seating wall if designed with a wide horizontal surface on top.

Retaining walls also have a specific purpose, since they are predominately designed to hold a significant load of soil. These walls should be engineered appropriately (depending on the size and complexity), factoring in lateral earth pressure. Walls connected to public infrastructure must be built for safety and stability, including those used in roads, harbours, dams, subways, railroads, tunnels, mines, and military fortifications (Dhamdhere et al., 2018).

Figure 5.1 shows a retaining wall connected to an overpass embankment along a trail corridor. Simple, yet cheerful flower paintings now cover up graffiti that had once made the area look run down. Since this is not a technical reference book, we'll leave the engineering discussion to experts more qualified. However, the stability of a retaining wall is equally important in relation to place-making. Cracks and minor structure failures can look dangerous and unkempt, and they can send messages that the area is uncared for.

The thickness of the wall or fence can determine stability and permeability. Thick walls that are built of dense, solid material like stone or brick, are often better able to block out or keep in sound, light, and

Figure 5.1 Cheerful flower paintings cover up graffiti on an overpass embankment.
Credit: Debra Cushing.

air. These are often more stable, but more costly. While thinner walls and those with gaps like wooden or chain-link fences may offer opportunities for permeability, affording visual access in and out, as well as the flow of air and/or water. It is important that the design suits the function of the barrier, and thought is given not only to the stability but also to human experience and perceptions.

In addition, as we highlight in our first book, *Creating Great Places* (Cushing & Miller, 2020), materials and design chosen should contribute to a sense of place and be appropriate for the area in which they are located. This will help the wall or fence fit in and contribute to the place – ideally creating a more remarkable experience. In Santa Fe, Arizona, for example, a thick apricot-coloured adobe wall with rounded edges looks natural and contributes to the sense of place. It fits. This style is functional and efficient, keeping the buildings cool in the hot summer, and warm in the winter. And it also provides fireproofing, sound buffering, and mould resistance, as well as other benefits. But that same wall would look strange in a humid, tropical environment where air flow is critical, and the colour of the earth is different than the burnt orange dessert soil in the SE part of the United States. Figure 5.2 shows examples of a typical adobe building in Sante Fe, New Mexico, and a wooden fence at a botanic garden that includes leaf shaped cut outs. Both contribute to the identity of their cultural and environmental context.

Similarly, the whitewashed walls synonymous with Greece and the Mediterranean first came about for practical reasons. The white paint helped cool the buildings in the summer months by reflecting sunlight. This is due to the albedo effect. Scientists and built environment

82 Unremarkable elements

Figure 5.2 Walls and fences that can contribute to place identity and sense of place.
Credit: Debra Cushing; Ken Lund (Flickr CC 2.0).

professionals today often pay attention to this due to the urban heat island effect, and the higher temperatures seen in urban areas as compared to regional or rural areas. White or light colours have a very high albedo rating because they reflect a majority of the solar radiation that hits the surface back into the atmosphere (UCAR, 2022). The surface albedo value is defined as the reflectivity, with a high number meaning greater reflectivity (Taha, 1997). Using high albedo materials, or those that are painted white in the case of white Mediterranean walls, reduces the solar radiation absorbed by buildings and urban spaces and keeps their surfaces cooler. This helps cool the planet, the buildings, and ideally the outdoor spaces adjacent to these walls.

Seeing green: green walls, green facades, and living walls

Green walls can also help mitigate the urban heat island effect and provide other benefits to a place. They can be classified into green façades, when plants are rooted at the ground-level and grow vertically; and living walls, when the substrate is vertically attached to the building (Susca et al., 2022). The shading and insulation properties of leaves can contribute reductions in temperature, especially in hotter climates. If you think about the ivy-covered walls in the United Kingdom and Northeastern United States, they can act as thermal shields to help with heating and cooling.

In addition, their impact also depends on plant characteristics, substrate properties, irrigation, plant albedo, plant biological activity, foliage density, weather and climate conditions, season, time of day, building dimensions, and orientation of the wall itself (Susca et al., 2022). As architectural facades, green walls need to be designed properly to avoid damage to the building. Function and stability need to be a priority to ensure public safety. But their value includes a host of benefits including noise reduction, ecosystem services, pollutant removal, and beautification, among others (Susca et al., 2022).

The systematic review of green wall research by Susca et al. (2022) showed that green walls generally lower the cooling and heating energy demand for buildings, although this varies across regions. Green walls show the best thermal performance in climate regions described as warm temperate, fully humid with warm summers, where they decreased building heating and cooling energy demand up to 16.5% and 50.6%, respectively. Similarly, research conducted in the hot, arid climate of Iran, found that a living wall system can reduce the ambient air temperature by up to 8.7°C (47.66°F) and can reduce temperature fluctuations by decreasing the maximum and increasing the minimum temperatures of the ambient air (Shafiee et al., 2020).

Green walls can also help us create biophilic cities and provide many psychological benefits for humans. See Figure 5.3 for an example of

Unremarkable elements

Figure 5.3 An example of a green wall in Denmark.
Credit: Loorzby (Flickr CC 2.0).

plants growing on the side of a building in Denmark. As discussed in our earlier book, *Creating Great Places* (Cushing & Miller, 2020), biophilic design is an important design theory that describes the innate human connection with nature and green spaces, and our love for living systems. Green walls can re-introduce green elements into our daily environments, including buildings and public spaces (Ignatieva & Ahrné, 2013). These elements provide opportunities for us to re-connect with natural processes and other living things. The calming and restorative impact that being close to nature within a heavily hardscaped urban environment may be significant and serves as a demonstration of Attention Restoration Theory (Kaplan, 1995) and Stress Recovery Theory (Ulrich et al., 1991). These effects were seen during an evaluation in school classrooms in a Dutch municipality close to Amsterdam that showed students with a green wall scored better on a test for selective attention and the green wall positively influenced classroom evaluations (Van den berg et al., 2017). But there was no measurable impact on processing speed or self-reported well-being.

Perhaps a simpler version of a green wall, a living hedge of shrubs or trees can often be an effective and beneficial barrier. Hedge rows and windbreaks have long been used in agriculture contexts to help control erosion or damage by wind. Living hedges, either natural or pruned and shaped, are often a solution in residential areas. Plant species such as Yews (*Taxus* spp.), Beech (*Fagus* spp.), and Boxwood (*Buxus* spp.) are commonly used in temperate climates in the northern hemisphere, such as the United Kingdom. Living hedges were often used in medieval gardens, as at the Powis Castle in Wales. And an article in the *Smithsonian Magazine* (2020) suggests that hedges have become the unofficial emblem of Great Britain, with the subtitle, 'A shear celebration of the ubiquitous boxy bushes that have defined the British landscape since the Bronze Age', with the opening line, 'Welcome to hedgeland'.

Although hedges are often joked about, Dr Tijana Blanuša, Principal Scientist with the Royal Horticultural Society, suggests that 'a "humble" hedge can provide so many benefits – protection from noise, improving air quality, reducing flooding risk and benefitting biodiversity' (RHS. UK, n.d.). For example, urban hedgerows are effective at reducing air pollution and roadside airborne particulates (Blanuša et al., 2020). They can also provide habitat for certain fauna and insect species, which can be an added benefit towards creating a sustainable urban environment.

Resistance or hesitation about implementing green walls can include concerns about the installation and ongoing maintenance costs. Some are actually not considered sustainable due to the increased resource requirements to keep the plants alive (Ignatieva & Ahrné, 2013). But with new techniques and innovations, this can change. As our urban environments become more and more grey, green walls may provide a good antidote.

Fences for more-than-human purposes

As mentioned at the start of this chapter, fences can be used to protect or control wildlife, and are installed to prevent the interaction between humans and animals. This includes domesticated pets like dogs, or wildlife species in urban areas. It is almost always the case that these interactions happen because humans have encroached on wildlife habitat through development. In order to prevent further impact, fences are often erected to help prevent unnecessary or detrimental conflicts.

However, in wildlife conservation circles, there is debate about the value of fences and the need to carefully evaluate their use (Woodroffe et al., 2014). And research is lacking on the large-scale and cumulative effects of fences and walls on a multitude of species and ecosystems (Jakes et al., 2018). For certain species, barriers can provide protection from predators, but they can also interrupt landscape connections and lead to habitat fragmentation, which may result in long term impacts. Within urban environments, which is the context for this book, habitat fragmentation is also due in large part to development and the destruction or alteration of habitat, in addition to fencing. But fencing plays a role, whether intentional or not.

Some local governments are requiring 'fauna friendly' fencing that attempts to limit disruption to animal movement or styles that could ensnare wildlife. This is not a one-size fits all type of fence and it needs to be designed according to the context and the specific species in the area. In places like Australia, wildlife such as koalas are often impacted by fencing that is erected around properties. They can get trapped in backyards if the fencing does not enable them to climb out. Many organisations have provided recommendations, including the simple use of coloured wire, tags or fabric that provide extra visibility for wildlife to perceive the fence.

The Queensland State Government, for example, has published *Koala Sensitive Design Guidelines* (2019) which recommends koala friendly fencing that allows koalas to easily climb under or through fencing, with a minimum gap of 300 mm (about 12 inches) between rails. Fences should be designed so that koalas can climb up, using wood or similar materials that a koala can grip, and with a minimum of 10 mm gap between vertical slats. However, fences that enable koalas to climb under is the best option, since they can easily become stuck in gaps that are not large enough. Exclusion fencing, that koalas cannot climb, should only be used within koala habitat in cases where there is a direct threat to the wildlife, such as near a busy road (see Chapter 6 on underpasses for a brief discussion on wildlife bridges over highways).

Why cheap or dilapidated walls and fences send a bad message

According to Broken Window Theory, it stands to reason that walls and fences that are not maintained and cared for, sends messages to users about the place and its value. Those that are constructed of cheap material or are not appropriate for their purpose and context, can easily become a blank canvas for offensive graffiti. Fences that are put up temporarily, and built with flimsy materials, can sometimes stay up for years and become eyesores, sending significant messages of neglect. Although walls and fences can be considered micro-elements of the urban environment, and are often mundane, overlooked, or treated as invisible, their design can have a significant impact.

Silt fences required on construction sites to control overland flows and sediment-laden stormwater, for example, can easily fail, allowing sediment to be washed into waterways (Whitman et al., 2021). Or they can stay up indefinitely when construction delays occur. Although performance is a concern since prefabricated silt fences are often perceived to perform poorly as a result of improper installation (Paterson, 1994),

Figure 5.4 Unique construction fencing that showcases Indigenous art on the Queensland University of Technology campus in Australia.

their aesthetics are also a consideration as well. Company logos are commonly printed on them, but other images, including artwork, are also a possibility. The construction fencing shown in Figure 5.4 has been designed using an Indigenous design from Queensland, Australia.

Walls and fences can easily decline in quality and appearance when left without maintenance. This is especially true for materials that deteriorate, such as timber. When neglected, they can collapse, develop broken rails and holes, become discoloured and faded, and generally look like they have not been maintained for some time. When they fall to this state, they may impact property values and the overall quality of the neighbourhood.

Material choice can also be a factor in how they are perceived. When the material looks out of place or is not maintained to the standard of the context, it can be perceived negatively. Barbed wire fencing is one example. Barbed wire was first introduced in 1893 in Illinois, USA to provide farmers and ranchers a fencing material to control livestock and delineate property boundaries (Bennett & Abbott, 2017). The negative and cruel implications on the health and safety of cattle and the ability for animals like buffalo to roam free are important to note, as are the social meanings associated with barbed wire. Barbed wire has also been used in military contexts and in places of control and oppression, like prisons and death camps. Given this cultural history, we often perceive barbed wire as a negative and wonder what is beyond that fence that we are not supposed to access.

Chain link fencing, sometimes used in combination with barbed wire, is another example. Although chain link doesn't have the intense negative connotations, it is difficult for it to positively add to the experience of a place. When chain link fencing is used around suburban residential properties, for example, it can look out of place and inappropriate.

88   Unremarkable elements

Fabric or mesh can be applied to it to provide privacy, but it is still a relatively low-quality option that is often purely functional.

Understanding how important fencing is to the perception and experience in our environment is important. Using the framework of cues to care, it is important to design walls and fences with purpose and an emphasis on how they can contribute to our urban environments. When designed well, walls and fences can maintain functionality, and provide essential messages about how the space is valued and people are experiencing it. In the next section, we look at two propositions for redesigning fencing to be more remarkable, with a focus on nudging sustainability and playability. We first look at sustainability with a green wall example in Singapore. We then turn to playability and propose that using DIY techniques like yarn bombing can add colour and fun to a drab urban environment.

Proposition 1: Nudging sustainability with green walls and vertical gardens

With its vision as the 'garden city' and its focus on clean and green landscapes (Newman, 2014), it is no surprise that one of the largest vertical gardens in the world is located in Singapore. The 24-story residential condominium complex called the Tree House, completed in 2013 by City Developments Limited, includes a vertical garden that covers 2,289 square meters.[1] The project received honours in the 'Best Innovative Green Building' category at the MIPIM Asia Awards 2013 and the vertical garden was listed in the Guinness World Records in 2014 as the largest green wall. Unfortunately, the world record was short lived, as it was surpassed in 2015 by the green wall created by the Cleanaway Company and Shine Green Energy to camouflage a landfill site in Taiwan.[2]

The green wall at the Tree House was designed as a 'bio-shield' to help mitigate the heat gain by the building by using lush plants as protection from the sun (Teo & Guatamo, n.d.). Located adjacent to Zhenghua Park that is connected to the larger Bukit Timah Nature Reserve, the green wall was envisioned to be an extension of the surrounding landscape as it climbs up the architectural façade. It is designed using a planter and climber model, with planters located every two stories, each with its own aluminium maintenance catwalk placed above the soil in the planters (Teo & Guatamo, n.d.). A rainwater harvesting tank on the roof collects water and then uses a gravity-powered automatic drip irrigation system to water the plants on the wall. Two climbing plant species dominate the wall: fast-growing *Thunbergia grandiflora*, known by the common name Blue Trumpet Vine, and slower-growing *Bauhina kockiana*, known as

Kock's Bauhinia or Red Trailing Bauhinia, with a third, *Quisqualis indica*, commonly called Rangoon Creeper, interspersed to enhance the butterfly habitat (Teo & Guatamo, n.d.).

In addition to Singapore's green open spaces and heavily landscaped streets, green walls are a way to create natural systems on building facades (Newman, 2014) which can increase biodiversity within the framework of biophilic urbanism. The Sky-Rise Greenery Initiatives programme run by the National Park Board in Singapore subsidises biophilic urbanism (Newman, 2014; National Parks Board, 2022). The programme promotes rooftop and vertical greenery and provides research, incentives, awards, and resources to support investment in green walls as one component of sustainable urban development. The BCA Greenmark scheme, established by the BCA Centre for Sustainable Buildings, also evaluates the sustainability of new developments.[3]

Many other green walls flourish in Singapore, with its tropical climate and its commitment to sustainability. While in other contexts, a green wall will require consideration of other factors more critically like irrigation and maintenance. Next, we switch to playability and using a DIY option to create more remarkable fences.

Proposition 2: Creating playable environments with yarn bombing on fences

Sometimes a DIY solution is all that is needed to create something remarkable. DIY options can be short or long-term solutions and can include simple options like fun paint colours and murals, or more complex interventions such as cutting window holes or using recycled materials to build the fence. The materials and design should fit the context and the purpose. And in many cases, a playful attitude is absolutely required.

One common DIY option is yarn bombing or applying colourful materials to a fence in a specific pattern or to create an image. Also referred to as yarn storming, graffiti knitting, and guerrilla knitting, it is considered the softer side of street art focusing both on aesthetics and making a statement with 'positive activism' (Haveri, 2016, p. 104). But it is not limited to fences.

Yarn bombers often create colourful knitted or crocheted sheaths to cover statues, tree trunks, phone booths, and other mundane elements in the public realm. Magda Sayeg, considered the woman who started yarn bombing in 2005, discusses yarn bombing: 'In this world of technology, over-development, fewer trees and more concrete, it is empowering to be able to beautify your environment' (Costa, 2010). Yarn bombers are often motivated by the opportunity to beautify a space to 'reclaim sterile urban environments and give them a personal

Figure 5.5 Simple hearts are attached to a chain link fence to add colour and life to a plain fence near a parking lot.
Credit: Sarah Nichols (Flickr 2.0).

touch' (McGovern, 2014, p. 1). Figure 5.5 shows a very simple example of yarn bombing on an otherwise drab chainlink fence.

Haveri (2016) reflects on the intent and message of yarn bombing:

> With the knitted graffiti the medium is the message. Yarn bombing brings soft human values and an ecological approach to replace the hard technologies of our time. The hectic rhythm of everyday life has given rise to cultural phenomena that emphasise slowness. There are concepts, such as slow food, slow design, slow cities and, of course, the super-ordinate term slow life. The growing popularity of crafts is related to this phenomenon. It challenges us to ask what good life is and what is valuable, real and enduring. Yarn bombers are telling this message.
>
> (p. 107)

Transforming a boring chain link fence around a school, or near a park, for example, is a way to create interest and have fun. As one example, the Sea Bright Knitting Club in New Jersey, USA, formed in the aftermath of Hurricane Sandy in 2012, took to yarn bombing their community to brighten it up after the destruction caused by the storm (Gurian, 2015). For their first project, the group decorated a fence on a street corner with brightly coloured knit grass, flowers, bees and butterflies.

Yarn bombing is a creative way to add a playful element to an urban space without a huge investment of resources. However, we note that yarn bombing is illegal if done on public property or without permission of the property owner. But as a friendlier form of graffiti and as it gets more popular, the artists and crafters are rarely policed (Haveri, 2016).

Conclusion

In this chapter, we argue for an alternate vision of walls and fences. The elements in our urban spaces typically used for 'blocking out' can be designed better in the future. Rather than seeing walls and fences as minute details that don't matter, designers need to embrace them as critical elements that can significantly impact how people (and wildlife) use space, how they perceive and interpret spaces, and how they live. It would be hard to imagine a contemporary urban environment without walls, fences and other forms of barricades, since they are ever present. We propose that these elements have unlimited potential to add value to the urban experience and can be designed to nudge healthier and more sustainable behaviours.

Notes

1 For more information about the green wall at the Tree House in Singapore, see https://cdl.com.sg/newsroom/cdl-sets-world-record-for-largest-vertical-garden.
2 See https://www.guinnessworldrecords.com/world-records/largest-vertical-garden-(green-wall)
3 For more information about the BCA Green Mark Scheme, see https://policy.asiapacificenergy.org/sites/default/files/Case-Study_The-BCA-Green-Mark-Scheme_A-Driver-for-Energy-Efficiency-Labelling-in-Singapore.pdf.

References

Bennett, L., & Abbott, S. (2017). *The perfect fence: Untangling the meanings of barbed wire*. Texas A&M University Press.

Biernacka, M., Kronenberg, J., & Łaszkiewicz, E. (2020). An integrated system of monitoring the availability, accessibility and attractiveness of urban parks and green squares, *Applied Geography*, 116, 1–16.

Blanuša, T., Qadir, Z., Kaur, A., Hadley, J., & Gush, M. (2020). Evaluating the effectiveness of urban hedges as air pollution barriers: Importance of sampling method, species characteristics and site location. *Environments*, 7, 81.

Costa, M. (2010). The graffiti knitting epidemic. *The Guardian*, Australia Edition. Downloaded 10 September 2022 from https://www.theguardian.com/artanddesign/2010/oct/10/graffiti-knitting

Cushing, D. & Miller, E. (2020). *Creating great places: Evidence-based urban design for health and wellbeing*. Routledge.

Davis, R., & Williams, E. (2008). Fences and between fences: Cultural, historical, and Smithsonian perspectives. *Journal of the Southwest*, *50*(3), 243–261.

Department of Environment and Science, State of Queensland. (2019). Environmental Planning and Policy, Koala-sensitive Design Guideline. A guide to Koala-sensitive design measures for planning and development activities. Downloaded 8 September 2022 from https://wildlifefriendlyfencing.org/wp-content/uploads/2022/05/Koala-Sensitive-Design-Guidelines.pdf

Dhamdhere, D. R., Rathi, D. V., & Kolase, P. K. (2018). Design and analysis of retaining wall. *International Journal of Management, Technology and Engineering*, *8*(9), 1246–1263.

Gurian, S. (2015). Profile: In storm-ravaged sea bright, Artist's Knitting Group is tie that binds. *NJ Spotlight News* (April 22, 2015). Downloaded 10 September 2022 from https://www.njspotlightnews.org/2015/04/15-04-21-profile-in-storm-ravaged-sea-bright-local-artist-s-knitting-group-is-the-tie-that-binds/

Haveri, M. (2016). Yarnbombing, the softer side of street art. In J. Ross (Ed.), *Routledge handbook of graffiti and street art* (pp. 103–112). Routledge.

Ignatieva, M., & Ahrné, K. (2013). Biodiverse green infrastructure for the 21st century: From 'green desert' of lawns to biophilic cities. *Journal of Architecture and Urbanism*, *37*(1), 1–9.

Jakes, A., Jones, P., Paige, C., Seidler, R., & Huijser, M. (2018). A fence runs through it: A call for greater attention to the influence of fences on wildlife and ecosystems. *Biological Conservation*, *227*, 310–318.

Kaplan, S. (1995). The restorative benefits of nature: Toward an integrative framework. *Journal of Environmental Psychology*, *15*, 169–182. https://doi.org/10.1016/0272-4944(95)90001-2

McGovern, A. (2014). Knit one, purl one: The mysteries of yarn bombing unravelled. *The Conversation*. Downloaded 10 September 2022 from https://theconversation.com/knit-one-purl-one-the-mysteries-of-yarn-bombing-unravelled-23461

National Parks Board. (2012). Skyrise Greenery Award. Singapore Government. Downloaded 8 September 2022 from http://www.skyrisegreenery.com/index.php

Newman, P. (2014). Biophilic urbanism: A case study on Singapore. *Australian Planner*, *51*(1), 47–65. https://doi.org/10.1080/07293682.2013.790832

Paterson, R. (1994). Construction practices: The good, the bad, and the ugly watershed protection techniques. *Ellicott City*, *1*(3), 44–48.

RHS.UK. (n.d.). Dr Tijana Blanusa. Tijana leads the Ecosystem Services Research Programme, identifying the structural and functional traits of plants that can be isolated, optimised and employed to benefit the wider environment. Downloaded 8 September 2022 from https://www.rhs.org.uk/science/meet-the-team/environmental-horticulture-team/tijana-blanusa

Robinson, P. (2007). 'Tear Down This Wall' how top advisers opposed Reagan's challenge to Gorbachev—But lost. Downloaded 8 September 2022 from https://www.archives.gov/publications/prologue/2007/summer/berlin.html

Shafiee, E., Faizi, M., Yazdanfar, S., & Khanmohammadi, M. (2020). Assessment of the effect of living wall systems on the improvement of the urban heat island phenomenon. *Building and Environment*, *181*, 1–12.

Susca, T., Zanghirella, F., Colasuonno, L., Del Fatto, V, (2022). Effect of green wall installation on urban heat island and building energy use: A climate-informed systematic literature review. *Renewable and Sustainable Energy Reviews*, *159*, 1–62.

Taha, H. (1997). Urban climates and heat islands: Albedo, evapotranspiration, and anthropogenic heat. *Energy and Buildings*, 25(2), 99–103.

Teo, A., & Guatamo, S. (n.d.). *Tree House condominium: Home with a green heart* (pp. 86–95). Downloaded 10 September 2022 from https://www.nparks.gov.sg/-/media/cuge/ebook/citygreen/cg10/cg10_tree_house_condominium.ashx?la=en&hash=C2359F2BD39D56D961040F43AA7E91B75DE906EC

UCAR Centre for Science Education. (2022). Downloaded 7 September 2022 from https://scied.ucar.edu/learning-zone/how-climate-works/albedo-and-climate#:~:text=Understanding%20how%20much%20energy%20from,the%20climate%20gets%20even%20cooler

Ulrich, R. S., Simons, R. F., Losito, B. D., Fiorito, E., Miles, M. A., & Zelson, M. (1991). Stress recovery during exposure to natural and urban environments. *Journal of Environmental Psychology*, 11, 201–230. https://doi.org/10.1016/S0272-4944(05)80184-7

Van den Berg, A. E., Wesselius, J. E., Maas, J., & Tanja-Dijkstra, K. (2017). Green walls for a restorative classroom environment: A controlled evaluation study. *Environment and Behavior*, 49(7), 791–813.

Whitman, J. B., Perez, Zech, W., & Donald, W. (2021). Practical silt fence design enhancements for effective dewatering and stability. *Journal of Irrigation and Drainage Engineering*, 147(1), 1–10.

Woodroffe, R., Hedges, S., & Durant, S. (2014). To fence or not to fence. *Science*, 344(6179), 46–48. https://www.science.org/doi/full/10.1126/science.1246251

Section II

Unremarkable spaces

6 Passing under

Redesigning underpasses to be more remarkable

Underpasses can be damp, dark, and dreary, with the deafening sounds of traffic overhead. The stench of urine and body odour, spoiled food, and garbage often fills the air. The leftover spaces under bridges and highway overpasses are notoriously underutilised in cities. Often devoid of a planned use, these spaces can become dumping grounds for household and industrial garbage. Even when not specifically dangerous, they can become attractive to rats, birds, and other wildlife, making them unattractive to people. Most people avoid them altogether or move through them quickly.

These are the spaces featured in suspense movies and detective shows as the site for homeless camps or drug deals, often with people gathered around a barrel fire for warmth. The grit of underpasses provides the backdrop in the movie 'Falling Down' starring Michael Douglas,[1] as a man who becomes unhinged in an LA traffic jam and abandons his car to walk towards an underpass embankment. And they are the places of loneliness and drug use, as described in the song, 'Under the Bridge', by the Red Hot Chili Peppers.

Artistic expression aside, underpasses often lack natural or regulated surveillance, becoming places to hide from public scrutiny. Frequented by transient people and squatters, they are ideal spaces for people who want to go undetected. And they provide a prime location for anti-social behaviour, such as drug activity and crime. If the activity becomes out of hand, or dangerous to others, police or other officials can take action to address the situation. The responses can be reactive to the immediate needs or can be proactive to address the systemic causes. Ideally both.

State officials in Austin, Texas, USA, for example, made headlines when the Texas Department of Transportation started clearing the homeless population from the underpasses of state highways in 2019 (Findell, 2019). Similarly, a tent city located in a Washington DC underpass was cleared due to danger, both for those squatting and those passing by. An excerpt from a *Washington Post* article

DOI: 10.4324/9781003052746-8

(Heim & Moyer, 2020) paints a picture of the increasingly common situation:

> … a dank and gloomy underpass connecting rapidly growing neighborhoods of high-end condos, gleaming office buildings and trendy restaurants. The rumble of trains pulling in and out of Union Station on the tracks above creates a steady din, and the blare of horns and sirens pierces all hours of the day. It often smells.
>
> The underpass is no place to call home, but home is what it's called by the several dozen men and women whose tents, blankets and belongings cover the sidewalk on both sides of the street. They've ended up here from nearby and far away.

Washington DC business district leaders tried to clear out encampments by filling an underpass with artistic light sculptures designed through an international design competition (Dvorak, 2019). However, one journalist writes about the clash commonly associated with gentrification, between the needs of the homeless population and the desires to clean up an area and make it more attractive to others, often people with money. The author rightfully questions whether simply adding art to the underpass will address the challenges of homelessness, commenting, 'To the homeless men and women who camp there, the underpasses are a no-brainer for safe and relatively dry shelter, now with décor' (Dvorak, 2019). The City of Houston, Texas, USA also addressed a similar issue with their homeless population, but instead set up safe low-level shelters in the underpasses and on private property. These professionally staffed spaces are fenced and sheltered, offering people a place to sleep on mats at night if they don't have any place to go (Thomas, 2017).

If we consider *Broken Window Theory*, these underpasses send significant messages. Once one person or group tags an underpass wall with graffiti, others follow suit. The impact can spread and build until the area is no longer considered safe or desirable. If a space under a bridge or highway becomes run down with peeling paint, weeds, and dripping water, it becomes a space that is no longer appealing for most people. Even if it does not become dangerous, it is considered an eyesore.

In this chapter, we are by no means advocating a quick fix or a band aid for complex social challenges, such as homelessness and drug use. Those are often systemic societal issues that need to be addressed more wholistically, with both policy and action. Cleaning up one underpass may just move the problem to another location. However, what we are advocating is to pay careful attention to these spaces in urban environments and think about how they can be made more remarkable.

Proper maintenance and drainage are easy first steps. Going beyond that by adding interesting or artistic lighting, applying colour or texture to enhance the aesthetics, playing with sound such as music that echoes, or adding healthy activities such as bridge runs, relay races and climbing walls, can greatly enhance their contribution to a sustainable, salutogenic, and playable environment. Or covering the underside of a bridge in a more sophisticated or aesthetically pleasing material can be effective, as was the case for Busbrug bridge in the Dutch city of Zwolle. Ipv Delft, the designers that created the Hovenring (see Chapter 10 for a description), designed the Busbrug with the underside clad in bamboo, providing a sophisticated covering to the bare concrete underside of the 245-meter concrete and steel structure (Reid, 2019). Taking inspiration from projects like this, we discuss why redesigning unremarkable underpasses can be important for creating an inviting and liveable city that is sustainable, salutogenic, and playable.

The purpose of underpasses

Bridges and highways are critical urban infrastructure. For cities to build up rather than out, underpasses are necessary to create a multilayered network with vertical separation for added safety and functionality. Overpasses, sometimes referred to as flyovers, help avoid conflicts between different types of uses. Separating pedestrians from cars, providing a way to cross over rivers or rail corridors, and enabling high-speed and high-volume traffic to skirt downtown areas, overpasses and underpasses are a common solution in urban situations. One use goes above, and one below.

Typically, planners, landscape architects, urban designers, and engineers determine which use is designated for the overpass versus the underpass. But it is not always that simple. Sometimes there is one primary use. A vehicle bridge over a canyon or river, for example, facilitates movement across a significant landscape feature that may be impassable otherwise. This means there can be leftover spaces under the bridge that are secondary in importance or are potentially unplanned. In some cases, people are not meant to use these secondary spaces other than for maintenance access.

However, when there is forethought, these spaces can be designed for multiple uses. This is not only efficient but adds to the value to the infrastructure itself. Because bridge and tunnel infrastructure are costly and resource intensive, it makes sense for them to be multiuse at the outset. When thinking about the left-over spaces that are not part of the primary use, key considerations such as location and access, community needs, and sense of place, should be raised – early in the design process.

Can underpasses be remarkable?

The simple answer is yes. From urban parks under highways with shade-loving plants, to skate parks that take advantage of the expanse of concrete and noisy location, to pop-up musical stages that incorporate the unique angles of highway foundations and support structures, this chapter highlights some of the unique ways that these spaces can be redesigned or simply re-used.

Take a stroll through New York City's Central Park and you see numerous arches and bridges that were designed (and currently maintained) with quality materials and care. As functional infrastructure, they significantly contribute to how people use and perceive of the park, adding variety, mystery and intrigue to the experience. Functionally, they separate uses, providing safety for horses, pedestrians and cyclists to stay away from cars. Aesthetically, they also contribute to the sense of place and overall character of the park. They add value to our experiences and our perceptions in that setting. This happens at an intimate human scale.

At a much larger scale, there are grand infrastructure projects that we can look to for inspiration. Heading south from NYs Central Park to Brooklyn, we find DUMBO. Once known as 'Fulton's Landing Area', it is now the popular area called DUMBO (Down Under the Manhattan Bridge Overpass). With incredible views of the iconic Manhattan bridge, including its underside, the area has capitalised on its unique location, between the Brooklyn and Manhattan bridges on the East River, opposite downtown Manhattan. It was previously an industrial district, with warehouses and factories, but in the late 1970s it became a residential area for artists living in inexpensive loft apartments. With increasing gentrification in 2007, the New York City Landmarks Preservation Commission voted unanimously to designate DUMBO as the city's 90th historic district. Also known as the centre of the Brooklyn Tech Triangle, it is now one of the most expensive areas to live in New York City (Rauscher, 2018). Not bad for an area underpass. In fact, its location 'under' the Manhattan Bridge, and its industrial heritage, are perhaps what makes it appealing as a space.

Two other examples of parks built under bridges or freeways include: the Bentway in Toronto, Ontario in Canada, and the Underline in Miami, Florida in the United States. Both projects are part of the Highline Network of infrastructure reuse projects.[2] The Bentway opened in 2018 and is located under the Gardiner Expressway along the shoreline of Lake Ontario. Developed by the Bentway Conservancy, the project importantly recognises that the site was a trade junction and a hunting and gathering place for Indigenous peoples, including the Mississaugas, the Haundenosaunee, the Huron-Wendat, the Metis and many others. The project received funding from a public-private partnership between the Under the Public Transit Infrastructure Fund and philanthropists Judy and Wilmot Matthews, who contributed $25 million to the project. The project was inspired by urbanist Ken Greenberg and landscape architecture firm PUBLIC WORK to re-imagine the site under the expressway. The project is considered a 'platform for creative practice, public art, and connected urban life' with year-round programming which includes a 220-meter looped figure-eight ice skating rink in the winter months.[3]

Similarly, the Underline in Miami is a 10-mile linear park, urban trail, and public art destination located under the Metrorail.[4] Phase one, called the Brickell Backyard, was designed by landscape architects at James Corner Field Operations and opened to the public in 2021. The design includes a procession of outdoor rooms that afford different activities, including the River Room, the Urban Gym, the Promenade, and the Oolite Room.

These massive, multi-phased infrastructure projects recognise the importance of function and context, as well as design quality and site programming to enhance the experience of a space. They also show that underpasses have huge potential. By affording new uses and focusing on the design of the underpass, we can add valuable public space options that are safer for everyone. The solutions can also be simple, with the addition of plantings, lighting and murals. If we think about *Cues to Care Theory*, providing symbols of legitimate use or indications of possible activities to people who are typically avoiding these leftover spaces, we can change how underpasses are perceived and used. We can make them more remarkable.

Design considerations

Considerations for the 'negative space' created under or near infrastructure include the height of the structure and overhead clearance, accessibility, visibility, location within the community, noise, and exposure to environmental elements, such as sunlight, run-off, and wind. In some cases, these site conditions offer opportunities for creative solutions. For example, the cool shade created under a bridge or highway can be a benefit in the hot summer to provide a prime location for physically demanding activities or to simply escape the hot summer sun. That is the case for a small urban plaza called Fish Lane Town Square in Brisbane, Australia located beneath railroad bridge infrastructure as shown in Figure 6.1. In other cases, these conditions present constraints on what can actually happen in that space. For example, if a space is hard to access or the clearance is very low, it might limit the options.

The design of these spaces is not always a high priority in terms of construction budgets, as they are often seen as residual space. Although

102 Unremarkable spaces

Figure 6.1 A lush urban plaza underneath railroad infrastructure, designed by RPS Group.
Credit: Debra Cushing.

they are commonly built with concrete, they can also be made from other materials such as steel, stone, and wood in conjunction with other facing materials. Depending on the span and weight limits of the bridge or overpass, other structural reinforcements are used. Materials not only help determine the aesthetic and ambiance created by the structure, but they can also influence the use.

Sound is a key consideration for underpasses. The typical clonk heard as cars drive across expansion joints on bridges is distinctive, if not annoying. Expansion joints are necessary for a bridge to flex slightly under environmental pressures, such as temperature variations and intense wind. Other noises can also be created by wind. The iconic Golden Gate Bridge in San Francisco, for example, experienced a loud humming noise that was compared to a 'ghostly harmonica', 'chanting monks' and a 'wheezing kazoo' (McCormick, 2021). Engineers determined that the sound can be heard when intense winds hit the aerodynamic railings at a specific angle. Although the railing slats were designed to withstand winds of more than 100 mph, the noise was something they didn't plan for.

Although the Golden Gate Bridge is an extreme example, echoes or noises emanating from bridges and overpasses can severely impact uses under and adjacent to a bridge. Sound absorbing screens and noise attenuation walls and barriers can often be seen along highways when they go through residential zones. However, these same techniques are not usually applied under bridges if they do not have a planned use.

Noise-mapping should be done to determine how much impact the traffic noise would have on any potential use. Noise pollution in urban areas is a relatively new area of policy and research. Environmental noise has been linked to detrimental health and well-being implications, including sleep disturbances, mental health impacts, and negative emotions such as anger, anxiety, unhappiness and disappointment (Murphy & King, 2010). Because of the significance of this issue, the European Union has created an Environmental Noise Directive[5] which requires strategic noise mapping to identify current or planned areas of noise situation in which the specified limits are breached, factoring in the number of people impacted. Although environmental noise is attributed to many factors such as road traffic and air traffic, studies have also focused on mitigation measures that can be used under bridges.

One experimental study found that the installation of sound-absorbing material on the vertical walls of an underpass did little to reduce noise levels, but that sound-absorbing pavement or sound-absorbing material applied to the under structure of the bridge may be more effective (Herman et al., 1999). Depending on the funding available and the source of the noise, other mitigation efforts may need to be sought. We also suggest that the type of use planned for these spaces should be considered. Temporary uses that only require passing through, or uses that have their own noise considerations, may be feasible options when noise mitigation is ineffective or prohibitively costly.

In some cases, the noise and conditions of an underpass could co-exist with other uses, without negative impacts. A case study on two flyovers in Kuala Lumpur Indonesia found that these spaces were the location of uses including food stalls and cafes, sports and recreation activities, such as pingpong and chess, and businesses, such as a car wash. In addition, less frequent activities such as twice-weekly evening food markets and cultural activities with traditional performances and music also occurred in those spaces (Qamaruz-Zaman et al., 2018).

More than human use of bridges and underpasses

Noise and traffic impacts are also considered in relation to wildlife bridges. The impact of urbanisation and densification on wildlife and ecological systems is extensive. One approach to minimise these impacts, is to make use of underpasses and bridges as wildlife corridors. These bridges, which include overpasses or underpasses to be used by wildlife, can provide ways to deal with conflicts between people and wildlife. From relatively large animals like deer, moose and kangaroo, to small animals and reptiles, like mice, toads, and lizards, wildlife bridges provide safe passage across busy roads. Although the ideal would always be to keep the habitat in one large area, sometimes the damage is done, and an alternative solution needs to be found. Any solution should also include empirical research to monitor and determine effectiveness.

Research on bats, for example, has shown that they will use underpasses if carefully aligned with pre-construction commuting routes that do not require a significant change in their flight height or direction. At one crossing in the United Kingdom, up to 96% of bats monitored flew through the underpass as opposed to crossing the road (Berthinussen & Altringham, 2012). Bat gantries, which are often pylon structures with netting or wire built to mimic trees and guide bats across roads at a safe height above traffic, were found to be essentially ineffective (Crowley, 2020).

A successful example of a well-studied wildlife bridge can be found in the Banff National Park managed by Parks Canada (Ford et al., 2009). Because of the research and policy initiatives undertaken by Parks Canada, the wildlife crossings along the Trans-Canada Highway have been monitored since 1983 and are among the most studied in the world. Different designs were incorporated, including exclusion fencing along stretches of the highway. Long-term monitoring results show that mammals present in the National Park such as deer, sheep, elk, bear, coyotes, wolves, lynx, fox, and cougars use the wildlife crossings, and the fencing has significantly decreased the number of wildlife/vehicle collisions, which increases motorist safety (Ford et al., 2009).

Nudging propositions: Redesigning underpasses to be more salutogenic and playable

In order to make underpasses more remarkable, we must rethink how they are used. Considering this at the outset, prior to construction, is ideal. Once they are already built, we need to take the opportunity to re-evaluate and redesign them. Here we discuss two propositions. The first looks at designing underpasses to afford skateboarding and similar activities to encourage physical activity in these spaces. The second focuses on play and how we can create more playable cities by adding murals and artwork in underpasses.

Proposition 1: Nudging skateboarding through a salutogenic approach to underpasses

With the abundance of concrete, the ambient noise from traffic, and the persistent shade from overhead structures, one use that might easily co-exist in these conditions is skateboarding. As a type of physical activity, skateboarding, along with inline skating, BMX biking, and scootering, are activities that can appeal to a younger population. Skateboarding can provide a healthy outlet that combines exercise with social engagement, but it c also be met with negative public perceptions.

Developed in the 1950s within the surfing community, skateboarding has gone in and out of favour. In the 1970s, skaters in urban areas often appropriated deserted swimming pools, drainage channels, and schoolyards for skateboarding (Chui, 2009). But the escalating complaints from the public and a perceived conflict with other urban uses led to the construction of fenced off skate parks in many cities across the United States and Europe. Then in the 1980s and early 1990s skateboarding expanded again into the streets, sidewalks and public spaces. To address this, places like New York City enacted a law restricting skateboarding on sidewalks and public plazas in 1996 and instead provided 16 designated skate parks around the city (Chiu, 2009). Although the designated skate parks may add legitimacy to the activity, research suggests that skateboarding is often considered an anti-social behaviour, with skaters labelled as 'noise makers, graffiti writers, and juvenile delinquents' (Chiu, 2009, p. 36).

Often considered an action sport, instead of a team sport, skateboarding is once again gaining ground as a legitimate and beneficial activity. It was designated as an official event at the 2020 Tokyo Summer Olympic Games and is becoming popular among both youth and adults. Regardless of which ages participate, it is extremely important that if underpasses are designed as skate parks, they need to be designed well and not seen as leftover spaces that no one wants. Like other spaces we discuss in this book, underpasses need to be functional, affording appropriate uses with cues that they are maintained and cared for in the urban environment. And if skateboarding is to become a more intergenerational activity, appealing to older age groups in addition to youth, the affordances need to be designed accordingly. Quite simply, underpasses need to be remarkable.

One well-known example can be found in Portland, Oregon. With its own Wikipedia page[6] and countless mentions on skater blogs, the Burnside Skatepark located under the east side of the Burnside Bridge in Portland is a popular example of a skate park built under a freeway. See Figure 6.2. Billed as one of the first DIY skate parks, it was started in 1990 by a group of skateboarders, including Bret Taylor, Chuck Willis and Osage Buffalo, who poured a concrete wall in an empty parking lot (Hamm, 2010). It grew from there and now features many hips, pools, pyramids and vertical sections. As is often the case with DIY placemaking initiatives, the skaters did not have permission from the city officials prior to constructing it. But given

Figure 6.2 Burnside Skatepark in Portland, Oregon.
Credit: Brad 061807 011 (Flickr CC).

its success, the Burnside Skatepark is now credited to have started the DIY skatepark movement inspiring other similar spaces. To date, it can be considered a successful redesign of an otherwise neglected urban underpass.

Proposition 2: Nudging play with murals and artwork

Underpasses and bridges offer blank canvases. Often constructed of concrete, with a utilitarian and functional façade, underpasses can afford space for murals created by local artists of community groups to help bring life and colour to a typically grey environment. Figure 6.3 shows an underpass with a water themed mural in Rockhampton, Australia.

One such example is the rainbow tunnel painted at the entrance to an underpass along the East Don Trail in Ontario. The mural can be seen on the east side of the Don Valley Parkway in Toronto as shown in Figure 6.4. Originally painted in 1971 by teenage artist B.C. Johnson who was known at the time as a guerrilla mural artist.[7] Johnson painted the mural as a tribute to his friend who was killed in a crash on the Parkway (Zettler, 2019). Although at times, the mural was removed by the city and tagged with graffiti by community members, it has withstood the test of time and has officially been restored twice by a non-profit team of mural artists. In addition, a second mural was

Figure 6.3 Water themed underpass in Rockhampton, Australia.
Credit: Evonne Miller.

painted on the inside of the tunnel in 2013 with local youth from Flemingdon Neighbourhood Services (Matejka, 2022).

For another example of using artwork within an underpass, we go to Netherlands. Highlighted in travel blogs and YouTube videos, the Silly Walks Tunnel (Dommel tunnel) in Eindhoven, Netherlands features

Figure 6.4 The Rainbow Tunnel in Toronto.
Credit: Dyniss Rainer (Flickr CC 2.0).

108   Unremarkable spaces

Figure 6.5 The Silly Walks Tunnel in the Netherlands.
Credit: PvL83 (Flickr CC).

black and white images of John Cleese, the star character in the Monty Python sketch 'Ministry of Silly Walks'.[8] See Figure 6.5. The mural was created by artists Niels van Swaemen & Kaspar van Leek from Studio Giftig in 2016[9] and features large silhouettes of Cleese demonstrating how to start, step, tread, gallop and use accessories like a briefcase, umbrella, or hat while passing through the pedestrian underpass near the central train station.

This mural is part of the City's Smile Factor initiative aimed at giving artists and creative residents a chance to work in their own city (Brunlett & Brunlett, 2018). The initiative is helping to enliven public spaces and celebrate artistic expression. Quoted in an online article, the Eindhoven alderman Yasin Torunoglu described the motivation for the mural (Wagenbuur, 2016):

> This Silly Walk fits perfectly into our new policy we call the smile factor. In which we try to give a new meaning to our public space.

As a city we can contribute by changing boring walls into a sort of fitness instruction for our citizens. I am looking forward to people walking into the tunnel with a gloomy face and walking out of it with a happy face …

Programmes such as these can be a great way to build a sense of community and connection and bring disadvantaged groups together to facilitate engagement and make a mark on the urban landscape. Children and youth, Indigenous groups, and others can be involved in mural programmes that give them a voice or enable them to display their artistic talents. Underpasses in need of colour and life, can provide a prime canvas on which to showcase these talents.

Conclusion

Once considered residual spaces and urban voids, the embankments and land under highway overpasses, railway bridges, and in tunnels can be transformed into enjoyable spaces that celebrate the unique infrastructure of urban environments. These residual spaces need to be considered in relation to their contribution to sustainable and healthy urban environments for all. With interesting microclimates due to almost constant shade and protection from the elements, they have huge potential. When cities have enough vision to make the most of these spaces, they can become special places. If a city can alter the reputation and use of these spaces by changing the design or simply adding small cues to show that they are not forgotten space, they can be celebrated. They can be more remarkable.

Notes

1 Read more about this film at https://www.imdb.com/title/tt0106856/.
2 See https://network.thehighline.org/resources/ for more information about the Highline Network.
3 See https://www.thebentway.ca/event/the-bentway-skate-trail-winter-season-2/.
4 See https://www.theunderline.org/ for more information about the Underline.
5 See https://environment.ec.europa.eu/topics/noise/environmental-noise-directive_en for more information about the European Union Noise Directive.
6 For more information about Burnside Skatepark see https://en.wikipedia.org/wiki/Burnside_Skatepark.
7 For more information, you can watch the YouTube video about Toronto's rainbow tunnel https://muralroutes.ca/mural/rainbow-tunnel/.
8 For more information about the Silly Walks Tunnel, see https://www.atlasobscura.com/places/silly-walks-tunnel.
9 For more information about Studio Giftig, see https://studiogiftig.nl/portfolio/murals/.

References

Berthinussen, A., & Altringham, J. (2012). Do bat gantries and underpasses help bats cross roads safely? *PLoS ONE, 7*(6), e38775. https://doi.org/10.1371/journal.pone.0038775

Brunlett, M., & Brunlett, C. (October 15, 2018). How to turn a car town into a cycling city: Lessons from the Dutch, where the number of bikes exceeds the number of people. *Next City online*. Downloaded 3 October 2022 from https://nextcity.org/features/how-to-turn-a-car-town-into-a-cycling-city

Chiu, C. (2009). Contestation and conformity: Street and park skateboarding in New York City public space. *Space and Culture, 12*(1), 25–42. https://doi.org/10.1177/1206331208325598

Crowley, J. (2020). Norwich NDR bat bridges 'are not working'. *BBC Inside Out East*. 26 January 2020. Downloaded 9 August 2021 from https://www.bbc.com/news/uk-england-norfolk-51193389

Dvorak, P. (2019). Battle of the D.C. underpass: Art parks vs. tent cities: The clash between the city's homeless population and wealthy newcomers is escalating (2 September 2019). *The Washington Post (Online)*. Downloaded 16 September 2022 from https://www.washingtonpost.com/local/battle-of-the-dc-underpass-art-parks-vs-tent-cities/2019/09/02/957213cc-cda5-11e9-87fa-8501a456c003_story.html

Findell, E. (2019). Texas begins clearing homeless from Austin underpasses (5 November 2019). *Dow Jones Institutional News*. Downloaded 12 September 2021 from https://gateway.library.qut.edu.au/login?url=https://www.proquest.com/wire-feeds/texas-begins-clearing-homeless-austin-underpasses/docview/2312124470/se-2?accountid=13380

Ford, A., Rettie, K., & Clevenger, A. (2009). Fostering ecosystem function through an international public–private partnership: A case study of wildlife mitigation measures along the trans-Canada Highway in Banff National Park, Alberta, Canada. *International Journal of Biodiversity Science & Management, 5*(4), 181–189. https://doi.org/10.1080/17451590903430153

Hamm, K. 2010, Burnside turns 20. *ESPN*. Retrieved 23 April 2015 from http://espn.go.com/action/skateboarding/news/story?id=5741014

Heim, J., & Moyer, J. W. (2020, Jan 12). Advocates decry order to clear homeless from underpass. *The Washington Post*. Retrieved from https://gateway.library.qut.edu.au/login?url=https://www.proquest.com/newspapers/advocates-decry-order-clear-homeless-underpass/docview/2335767711/se-2?accountid=13380

Herman, L. A., Seshadri, S. R., & Pinckney, E. (1999). Placement of sound-absorbing materials to control traffic noise reflections at a highway underpass. *Transportation Research Record, 1670*(1), 69–75. https://doi.org/10.3141/1670-09

Matejka, R. (2022). Rainbow Tunnel. *Mural Map of Canada*. Download 3 October 2022 from https://muralroutes.ca/mural/rainbow-tunnel/

McCormick, E. (2021). The quest to solve the mysterious 'eerie' hum of the Golden Gate Bridge. *The Guardian*, Australian Edition. Downloaded 26 September 2022 from https://www.theguardian.com/us-news/2021/jun/13/golden-gate-bridge-hum-noise-san-francisco

Murphy, E., & King, E. (2010). Strategic environmental noise mapping: Methodological issues concerning the implementation of the EU environmental noise directive and their policy implications. *Environment International, 36*(3), 290–298.

Qamaruz-Zaman, N., Samadi, Z., & Azhari, N. F. N. (2018). Under the flyovers of Kuala Lumpur: User centered activities in leftover spaces. *Journal of ASIAN Behavioural Studies, 3*(7), 141–151.

Rauscher, R. C. (2018). DUMBO and sustainable city principles. In: *New York neighborhoods – Addressing sustainable city principles*. Springer. https://doi.org/10.1007/978-3-319-60480-0_6

Reid, C. (2019). Maker of world's most iconic bicyclist bridge designs Bamboo-Clad Bus Bridge. *Forbes online*. (June 9, 2019). Downloaded 3 October 2022 from https://www.forbes.com/sites/carltonreid/2019/06/09/maker-of-worlds-most-iconic-bicyclist-bridge-designs-bamboo-clad-bus-bridge/?sh=7a5516d237fe

Thomas, K. E. (Mar 3, 2017). New Houston homeless plan targets underpass shelters. *Next City.Org*. Retrieved from https://gateway.library.qut.edu.au/login?url=https://www.proquest.com/magazines/new-houston-homeless-plan-targets-underpass/docview/1874061144/se-2?accountid=13380

Wagenbuur, M. (June 14, 2016). And now for something completely different. *Bicycle Duthc.com*. Downloaded 3 October 2022 from https://bicycledutch.wordpress.com/2016/06/14/and-now-for-something-completely-different/

Zettler, M. (June 20, 2019). YYZ Why? Toronto's Rainbow Tunnel on the northbound DVP. *Global News*. Downloaded 3 October 2022 from https://globalnews.ca/news/5414727/rainbow-tunnel-toronto-dvp/

7 Strolling along

Redesigning streets and sidewalks to be more remarkable

The COVID-19 pandemic has changed many factors of everyday life, including how people engage with and use streets and sidewalks. Lockdowns and the temporary closure of workplaces, schools, shopping centres, gyms, and playgrounds saw people turn to local streets for exercise and to engage in safe, physically distanced walking and bicycling. Citizen-led initiatives transformed streets and sidewalks, with people drawing in chalk fun games such as hopscotch, exercise activities, rainbows, trivia questions, and encouraging messages ('we're all in this together') and – inspired by the popular children's book *'we're going on a bear hunt'* – putting teddy bears in house windows, trees, and fences, to entertain and connect people during their walks around their neighbourhood. We see this in Figure 7.1, which shows teddy bears in trees and a chalk hopscotch in suburban Brisbane, Australia, during COVID-19. Globally, streets were transformed and reclaimed during COVID, into 'slow streets' with walking and biking prioritised (Fields & Renne, 2021); the degree to which changes will be sustained is debatable, but the move towards active transportation can benefit public health, urban congestion, and the overall liveability of our cities.

Streets and sidewalks are the ultimate places of movement: people, in cars, on bikes, public transport, or on foot, are on the move, from one place to the next. They have a simple physical form: a linear space with a connective function which provides a route, path, or space through which people travel. The street stretches from building edge to building edge, or property line to property line, and includes the sidewalk – which is a walking path within the street which comprises of four planes: *a ground plane, a canopy, a roadside, and a building side* (City of New York, 2010; Lynch, 1960). Unfortunately, as we see in Figure 7.2, streets and sidewalks can be poorly designed: even in the capital city of Brisbane, in Queensland, Australia, the sidewalk and bike path also abruptly end in an inner-urban suburb less than 2 km from the CBD. These photographs illustrate the importance of street and sidewalk design decisions, which can negatively impede movement and active travel.

DOI: 10.4324/9781003052746-9

Figure 7.1 Connecting during COVID-19 – chalk hopscotch and teddy bears in trees.
Credit: Evonne Miller.

The evolving role and design of streets: from streets for cars to streets for people!

The physical form and role of streets has changed significantly over the last few decades, as awareness has grown about their importance in community life. Their design has evolved – from being car-dominant to being much more people-friendly. *Liveable streets, complete streets, streets for all, shared streets, sticky streets, walkable cities*, whatever the precise phrase or terminology guiding this change, the central argument is the same: we must redesign and reinvest in our streets, providing *both* critical public spaces for people alongside pathways for traffic.

While streets comprise most of urban public space, historically they were designed for automobile movement and safety, providing wide lanes for traffic and little space for people. Thanks to the advocacy of organisations such as the National Association of City Transportation Officials (NACTO) and Project for Public Spaces (PPS), there is now a strong global movement advocating for a different vision for this critical public asset. Urban planners and designers, engineers, and communities are collaborating to redesign our streets to be 'for the people', not 'for cars'.

A large body of research literature and public policy initiatives demonstrates how well-designed streets can create a strong sense of

114 Unremarkable spaces

Figure 7.2 When streets and sidewalks are unremarkable in design.
Credit: Brent O'Neill; Michael Langdon; Anna Campbell.

place and community, fostering social connections and physical activity, and enhancing safety, health, mobility, and quality of life for all users: pedestrians *and* drivers. If you are tasked with redesigning a street to be more people-friendly, there are many invaluable online resources which outline tangible design strategies and best practice case studies.

The Global Street Design Guide (2016),[1] produced by the NACTO and the Global Designing Cities Initiative, outlines how to design urban streets for shared multimodality where people can safely walk, bike, take public transport and socialise, while the City of New York's (2010) Active Design Guidelines focuses specifically on redesigning the *sidewalk* experience. As they explain, sidewalks are key to healthy, sustainable, and resilient communities, acting as the connective tissue of neighbourhoods:

> Many factors contribute to creating a "walkable city" but the most important, and arguably the most neglected, is the design of the sidewalk. More than simply a concrete apron to mediate between road and building, the sidewalk is the stage on which pedestrian life plays out. It is the floor for the pedestrian "room" and as such deserves as much design attention as the living room of a home. A well designed sidewalk can make a street pleasurable and safe to walk down. A poorly designed sidewalk can be a deterrent to pedestrian traffic.
>
> (City of New York, 2010, p. 5)

In this chapter, after documenting the rationale behind the changing role and design of streets, we outline how the lens of salutogensis, sustainability, and play provides a valuable frame for redesigning streets to be remarkable.

Streets as places: placemaking and the Project for Public Spaces (PPS)

At this juncture, it is important to reflect on how streets are public places – which will only thrive if people chose to utilise them (Carmona et al., 2010). Thus, in rethinking streets and sidewalks to be places, we can draw inspiration from the influential United States based non-profit, *Project for Public Spaces* (PPS) which inspires world-best practice in place-making: both a process and philosophy, placemaking is about creatively reshaping space to be more engaging, authentic, and useable, thus generating a sense of places. Alongside helpful tools such as 'Power of 10' and Place Diagram,[2] the PPS have also identified eight principles for turning *streets as places*: (1) Great activities and destinations; (2) Safe; (3) Inviting and rich in detail; (4) Designed for lingering; (5) Interactive and social; (6) Unique; (7) Accessible; and (8) Flexible. While the costs of implementing these principles and creating great streets differs depending upon the desired changes and local conditions, fortunately, many interim and potentially longer-term street design strategies can be implemented quickly without significant costs, thus immediately demonstrating the value to users.

116 Unremarkable spaces

Transforming unremarkable streets – from park(ing) day, 'parklets', and 'right-sizing'

A relatively easy first step towards creating more people-friendly streets is to transform street parking spaces into small people places, either temporarily or permanently. This is the aim of Park(ing) Day,[3] which originated in San Francisco in 2005 as a do-it-yourself (DIY) approach to turning under-appreciated land use types – parking spaces – into exciting mini-green spaces for social connections. From these humble origins, where friends found and rented a parking space in a very urban part of downtown San Francisco, rolling out fake green grass, alongside a bench and large potted tree, Parking Day is now a global movement that engages communities in an ongoing dialogue about how we design and live in our cities.

The Park(ing) Day website outlines some exciting planned installations: the Oneida Improvement Committee, for example, will call their Park(ing) Day installation Bark(ing) Day, turning two parking spots into a play area for dogs; the Twist and Shout School of Performing Arts will turn a downtown Chicago parking lot into a giant life-sized game of chess; and on Rhode Island, an oversized loom will prompt passerbys to be part of Looking Upward's collaborative weaving project using recycled materials.

The success of Park(ing) Day motivated San Francisco's Pavement to Parks programme, which create 'parklets': more permanent Park(ing) style installations, usually sponsored by local businesses, that transform two to three parking spaces in a street into spaces for people to relax, connect and enjoy the city around them. This welcoming new public space typically features landscaping, benches, café tables and chairs, and bike parking. COVID-19 has also seen the creation of 'streatery', sometimes spelled streetery; combing the words 'street' and 'eat', 'streatery' is outdoor restaurant seating located in a space previously dedicated to vehicles, such as a street parking spot, lanes or parking lot. Figure 7.3 shows in a development 'streatery', in a street parking spot in the laneways of Melbourne, Australia.

While parking day, parklets, and streateries are relatively small-scale initiatives with big impact, larger macro-changes to streets are extremely influential. Changes to the existing building envelope of a street – from adjusting their width, edges, layout, orientation, structure, and typology, to moving curbs, reducing lanes and speeds, redirecting traffic, and adding buffers (between pedestrians, bikes, and vehicular traffic) and crossing medians for pedestrians – are relatively simple changes that can significantly improve road and pedestrian safety. The PPS describe how, in 2006, Charlotte in North Carolina begin the process of 'right-sizing' (reconfiguring

Figure 7.3 A streatery in street parking in Melbourne.
Credit: Evonne Miller.

the layout)[4] a large arterial street – East Boulevard[5] – with daily motorised vehicle traffic of 16,000–21,000. After introducing traffic calming measures and reducing vehicle lanes (from 5 to 3) which created space for bicycle and pedestrian space (bike lanes and 12 mid-block pedestrian refuge islands), vehicle speed reduced and road safety improved. Table 7.1 outlines some common urban traffic calming and pedestrian-priority street redesign strategies that are inexpensive and easily deployable.

Regardless of the size of the proposed change, critical to the street redesign process is engaging with local stakeholders to develop a shared vision of the look, feel, design, and experience of this street. Engagement and communication is essential to ensuring long-term success, so partnering with local residents, along with local businesses, advocacy groups, and government agencies (planning, development, transportation, public health, environmental) will help in the identification of key local issues, users, and priorities. A detailed and collaborative site analysis will help identify specific user groups and unique destinations (schools, aged care, playgrounds), thus informing the specific priorities for redesigning this street. In the next section, we argue that alongside engagement strategies and a traditional site analysis, designers should engage in a creative theory-storming process

118   **Unremarkable spaces**

Table 7.1 Inexpensive and easily deployable traffic calming and pedestrian-priority street design strategies

Modular Curbs: Streets can be transformed overnight by installing small concrete dividers, which reflect the desired configurations, without expensive or permanent infrastructure.

Flexible Bollards: These plastic delineators, easy to install and remove, direct traffic flows and reduce speed.

Paint and Thermoplastic Surface Materials: while not a physical barrier, paint can be applied quickly and relatively inexpensively, acting as a visual device that forces drivers to slow down and give way to pedestrians.

Planters: Inexpensive installations, planters add aesthetically pleasing vegetation and greenery to streets, which separate and define medians, curb extensions, islands, plazas, footpaths, and cycle tracks.

Temporary Site Interventions: Extremely effective tools for public engagement, these help street users visualise alternate uses of the street space, and may be implemented for hours, a day or weeks (e.g. Parking Day).

Sidewalk Widening and Intersection Redesign: Interim materials (gravel, paint, planter beds, bollards), can ease pedestrian congestion with interim markings changing the geometry of an intersection, calming traffic.

Source: Global Street Design Guidelines.

to explicitly consider how our streets might look different if a lens of salutogenic, sustainability, playable, and inclusive design is applied.

Proposition 1: Nudging health through salutogenic street design

Creating streets that are salutogenic, that is health promoting, has never been more important. Statistics from the World Health Organization show that, globally, obesity has tripled since 1975: 39% of adults aged 18 years and over are overweight, with 13% obese (WHO, 2021). In explaining why, researchers point to the fact that we live in obesogenic environments, where inactivity and overeating is encouraged. One key public health strategy is to redesign streets so that they foster active transportation and people are encouraged to engage in incidental physical activity (walking, biking) as part of daily life. This is powerfully illustrated in the scenario below, where through a protagonist they name Phil, Parikh and Parikh (2018) show how our urban environment impacts health decisions:

> Let's say Phil is about to set off to work on a spring morning. He can either walk or take the bus. These options may be compactly expressed by the set choices = {walk, take the bus}. What might induce him to walk, which is obviously better for his health but

takes more time and effort? Many things could influence him: whether he is late for work or it is raining, whether he plans to go to the gym later in the day, and so on. But all designers and architects are likely to concur that if there are no extraneous factors, a more inviting walking experience would nudge him toward walking.

(2018, p. 6)

Parikh and Parikh argue that Phil (and all of us) will be more likely to take the healthier option of walking *if the street is engaging, charming and 'cheerful'*. Thinking thoughtfully about the design of streets is extremely important, with research consistently linking the walkability of the built environment – the degree to which streets and sidewalks are accessible, connected and close to destination points (public transport, retail, schools, parks, playgrounds), safe, comfortable, shaded, attractive, and well-maintained – with active health behaviours (Baobeid et al., 2021; Patuano et al., 2022). While walking and cycling are environment-friendly and healthy urban transport modes, the reality is if it is unsafe or perceived to be too difficult, then people will drive. Purpose-built cycle ways, as we will see in the next chapter help; unfortunately, all too often, cycle lanes are squeezed into the existing road network – and simply painting a lane onto a road is not sufficient to encourage people to start cycling to work or the shops, if they have to also battle traffic and safety concerns.

Why we must green our streets: the health benefits of nature

One of the most critical aspects of a salutogenic street is the presence of urban greenery, which impacts the attractiveness, safety, perceived quality, appeal, and walkability of the environment. People more actually likely to walk or cycle if the streets are green spaces (Nawrath et al., 2019), with Ku and colleagues the first to show that the presence of vegetation in urban settings reduced rates of domestic violence and crime (e.g. Kuo & Sullivan, 2001). A wealth of research literature highlights the importance of 'greening' cities and nature-based solutions for our mental and physical well-being, as well as the environmental sustainability of our planet (see Beatley, 2010, for a detailed discussion on the value of biophilic cities).

Indeed, the presence (or not) of street trees has been linked to the prescription of antidepressants: looking at 31 districts across London, Taylor et al. (2015) linked higher density of street trees with fewer antidepressant prescriptions, with research in Germany also reporting lower rate of antidepressant prescriptions for people (especially those of low socio-economic status) living within 100 m of higher density of street trees (Marselle et al., 2020). As unintentional daily contact with nature benefits physical and mental health, whether it is street trees, permanent

120 Unremarkable spaces

parklets, or adding vegetation to street infrastructure (such as roadside vegetation, urban vertical gardens on bus stops and green living walls on buildings), we must make our urban streetscapes greener.

Proposition 2: Nudging play through the design of streets

A second key strategy to encourage people to engage and interact with their streets is through applying playable design principles, and to think in a creative manner about the multiple roles, experiences, sights, sounds, smells, and dimensions of our streetscapes. There are inspiring examples across the globe of playable streets, interactions, and experiences. Silent Lights, an urban art installation, has transformed an overlooked pedestrian pathway under Brooklyn's Queens Expressway into a playful space: the gates are embedded with 2,400 LED lights, with sound equipment transforming noise from the street into interesting light patterns.

Taking a different tack, the creators of the Walk Your City trial app in Graz, Austria proposed a different way to motivate users to walk and discover beautiful hidden spaces of the city: users would be rewarded with tokens, which would then be invested into desired improvements – such as parking benches or zebra crossings. While still in development, this idea uniquely combines play with gamification and physical activity, and it is such initiatives that help activate our public spaces. Similarly, the 'walking' school bus initiative – where groups of children are led to and from school, chaperoned by adults while walking – has also been shown to increase active commuting to school and rates of daily moderate-to-vigorous physical activity (Mendoza et al., 2011).

Imagine, however, the experience if *play* was intentionally integrated into the walk to and from school. What if interactive physical installations on the sidewalk encouraged an interactive game of 'eye spy' to spot hidden fairies, dragons, or animal sculptures, or if children and their parents could pause to create a melody on musical swings or a game of Tetris on an interactive rubbish bin. The streetscape could become a history trail, with significant markers at each location encouraging the sharing of memories, or perhaps a learning trail, with weekly spelling words, mathematics challenges or jokes integrated into interactive billboards. As we have discussed elsewhere (see Miller & Cushing, 2021), playable design can and should be used to nudge active, healthier choices, such as walking (not driving) to school.

Integrating public art in streetscapes

One way to record, remember and bring urban histories to life in streetscapes is through public art, which can reveal the unique character and values of a specific local site. Done well, meaningful, engaging, and high-quality public art can facilitate a sense of place and civic pride. Importantly, while many people do not visit art galleries or museums or the theatre, all people are able to experience public art. For example, San Francisco, the city that pioneered parklets, introduced Living Innovation Zones (LIZ) in 2013 to activate and invigorate their streets, through temporary interactive art and science installations that engage, delight, and prompt meaningful human engagement in public space – turning 'a sad sidewalk' into an interactive showcase of art and science.

Street pianos: making music part of our urban life

Street pianos are an often-cited example of playful placemaking, with the playful piano stairs example discussed earlier. First originating in 2008 in Birmingham in the United Kingdom, artist Luke Jerram placed 15 pianos in locations across the city for three weeks with the motto '*Play me, I'm Yours*' imprinted on them. Changing the dynamics of a space, and acting as a catalyst for conversation and connections, Street Pianos '*provoke people into engaging, activating and claiming ownership of their urban landscape*', with more than 2,000 pianos on 65 cities, played and listened by more than 20 million people worldwide.[6] The short film, *The People's Piano*,[7] documents the trans-formative impact of street pianos: as well as being environmentally responsible (hundreds of pianos are dumped each year), the process of making music brings unexpected joy and fun to often soulless places.

Sweeney et al. (2018) recently described the street piano experience in the post-industrial city of Newcastle, in Australia. This community-driven placemaking initiative, labelled Keys to the City, was started by a local artist and his son, and supported financially and admin-istratively by the local business improvement association and, logis-tically, by the city council. Despite some logistical challenges (one piano was destroyed by people and another by rain), the project has successfully activated the urban spaces and streets in new ways, even becoming part of a roving jam session when friends organised a public 'piano crawl'. While the installation and maintenance of street pianos requires ongoing effort, they serve as a powerful artefact that impli-citly remind people that this place is (1) their space and (2) playable.

> Even before a hand is laid upon the keys, the piano is an agential artefact. The pianos themselves are a quiet presence within the city-scape until they are played, but they are a presence, and an active one; their cleaned-up, retuned, hopeful existence in the everyday urban environment provokes a redefining of the socio-material landscape in ways both tangible and imaginary.
>
> (Sweeney et al., 2018, p. 12)

Proposition 3: Nudging sustainability, through the design and use of streets

Finally, the design and use of streets can nudge sustainability. As climate change impacts our cities, we must consider how to make the topological and morphological properties of our streets more sustainable. Whether it is the purposeful inclusion of parklets and 'green' parking spaces and lots, which foster sustainable urban drainage (SUD) by naturally filtering and mitigating surface water runoff, including pockets of urban greenery is a must do in the design of streets and sidewalks (see Chapter 9 for a further discussion of innovative sustainable design of parking lots, including raingardens for stormwater runoff). While a detailed examination is beyond the scope of this chapter and book, the geometry, orientation, and composition of a street influences both the pedestrian microclimate and broader planetary health. Fields and Renne's (2021) adaptation urbanism framework positions streets as key to climate mitigation and adaptation, proposing a new street design matrix focused on 'safety, spatial efficiency, equitability, community livability, and limiting GHG emissions' (p. 57). In their typology of streets of the past versus streets of the future, Fields and Renne predict that – with political will, change agents and thoughtful design – the 'great street of the climate change era' (p. 14) will be a carbon mitigator.

The sustainable use of streets: the rise of micro-mobility devices

Alongside purposely designing our streets to be sustainable, we can also rethink how we use them. One of the significant recent changes in how we use our streets is the rise of low powered electric micro-mobility devices: rental e-scooters and bicycles. Whether you love or hate them, these micro-mobility devices are increasingly part of our streetscape and transport network, viewed as an alternative strategy for reducing traffic congestion and getting people out of cars for short trips, the so-called *'first-and-last mile'*.

In America, the Portland Bureau of Transportation recently ran a pilot scheme to assess if e-scooters – by 'moving people efficiently in a climate-friendly way' (2019, p. 2) – could advance the city's goals for mobility, climate, equity, and safety. This trial found that e-scooters replaced 37% of car travel and 58% of low-carbon mobility modes (walking, biking, public transport, or not going) for locals. By shifting trips away from private motor vehicle use, as well as reducing traffic congestion and air pollution, the provision of scooters can also expand mobility and inclusion. As one survey respondent explained, 'as a person without the money for a car and a knee injury which prevents biking, e-scooters have opened a whole new world to me' (2019, p. 33). Oregon state law prohibits riding e-scooters on sidewalks, with the pilot reporting that safe infrastructure was critical to usage: mobility data showed that e-scooter use increased dramatically, between 22% and 125% at two different sites, after the introduction of protected bike lanes.

Portland, like many cities across the globe, recommended a permanent e-scooter programme. Micro-mobility devices are clearly changing the usability and experience of our streets, however as regulations and market behaviour evolves, their safe integration into existing transport systems has not been straight forward. While all modes of transport carry safety risks, as well as accidents while driving, there are many examples of e-scooter littering and people falling over them. In fact, in response to safety concerns, at the time of writing, several cities (e.g. Sydney in Australia) and countries (e.g. Singapore and France) have banned e-transport or revoked licenses, after accidents, injuries, and deaths. However, the most recent statistics show that e-scooters are in fact safer than driving cars: in 2020, in Great Britain,[8] 1,460 people were killed in road accidents (with 23,529 serious injuries), compared to 3 deaths from e-scooters (with 931 serious injuries). While hospital emergency departments report growing numbers of e-scooter injuries, impact assessments that allow micro-mobility devices argue that the benefits – both mobility and environmental – outweigh the social cost of injury.

So, just how environmentally friendly are e-scooters? In one of the first studies to focus on their entire environmental life cycle, Hollingsworth et al. (2019) – in their amusingly titled paper, *Are e-scooters polluters?* – examined their materials and manufacturing, collection and distribution, charging, and disposal, as well as daily usage and data on transportation modes being displaced. Unfortunately, as Hollingsworth et al. explain, when a life cycle lens is applied, the environmental argument is not as strong:

> While e-scooters may be an effective solution to urban congestion and last-mile problem, they do not necessarily reduce environmental impacts from the transportation system… Claims of environmental benefits from their use should be met with skepticism unless longer product lifetimes, reduced materials burdens, and reduced e-scooter collection and distribution impacts are achieved.
>
> (Hollingsworth et al., 2019, np)

As well as questioning their environmental impact, questions have arisen about the mobility and inclusion narrative of micro-mobility devices. While a detailed analysis is beyond the scope of this chapter, there is no doubt that new social norms and built forms will be needed to help ensure the safe operation of micro-mobility devices. One of the greatest challenges is their location and parking: In response, 'bird cages' – spray paint parking for electric scooters – has emerged as a solution to try and minimise their negative impact on our urban landscape. As micromobility continues to disrupt the traditional transport system and our streets, we must ensure our built form and systems responds in a way that fosters both social and environmental sustainability.

Conclusion

In closing, it is timely to consider both where we have come from and where we are heading in terms of street design. Over forty years ago now, in his 1981 book *Livable Streets*, Donald Appleyard challenged us all to 'raise our sights for the moment. What could a residential street—a street on which our children are brought up, adults live, and old people spend their last days—what could such a street be like?' (p. 243).

While there is no doubt that we have made significant progress over the last few decades, improving the design and experience of our streets, there is still significant room for improvement, in the design of new streets and the purposeful retrofitting of old streets. At their best, streets and sidewalks are interconnected, interesting, inclusive, exciting, and inviting, encouraging people to linger and connect. Like Appleyard, then, our challenge to readers is simple: if we are to truly create great places, and redesign the unremarkable, each of us needs to advocate for change. Whether it is actively participating in local community meetings about the master planning vision for your area or integrating playable design features into your next design proposal, each of us must help make our streets more remarkable.

Notes

1 See https://globaldesigningcities.org/publication/global-street-design-guide/
2 See https://www.pps.org/
3 See https://www.myparkingday.org/ Created by art and design collective, Rebar.
4 For a guide, see https://www.pps.org/article/rightsizing
5 See https://www.pps.org/article/8-principles-streets-as-places
6 See http://www.streetpianos.com/about/
7 See http://www.streetpianos.com/about/
8 Note, this was during COVID lockdowns, when road usage was down ~20%.

References

Appleyard, D. (1981). *Livable streets*. University of California Press.
Baobeid, A., Koç, M., & Al-Ghamdi, S. (2021). Walkability and its relationships with health, sustainability, and livability: Elements of physical environment and evaluation frameworks. *Frontiers of Built Environment*, 7, 721218.

Beatley, T. (2010). *Biophilic cities: Integrating nature into urban design and planning*. Island Press.

Carmona, M., Heath, T., Oc, T., & Tiesdell, T. (2010). *Public places urban spaces*. Taylor & Francis.

City of New York. (2010). *Active design: Shaping the sidewalk experience*. Accessed from: https://nacto.org/docs/usdg/active_design_shaping_the_sidewalk_experience_nycdot.pdf.

Fields, B., & Renne, J. (2021). *Adaptation urbanism and resilient communities: Transforming streets to address climate change*. Routledge.

Global Street Design Guide (2016). *Global street design guide: Global designing cities initiative*. National Association of City Transportation Officials. Island Press.

Hollingsworth, J., Copeland, B., & Johnson, J. (2019). Are e-scooters polluters? The environmental impacts of shared dockless electric scooters. *Environmental Research Letters*, 14(8), 084031.

Kuo, F., & Sullivan, W. (2001). Environment and crime in the inner city: Does vegetation reduce crime? *Environment and Behavior*, 33, 343–367.

Lynch, K. (1960). *The image of the city*. MIT Press.

Marselle, M. R., Bowler, D. E., Watzema, J., Eichenberg, D., Kirsten, T., & Bonn, A. (2020). Urban street tree biodiversity and antidepressant prescriptions. *Scientific Reports*, 10, 22445.

Mendoza, J., Watson, K., Baranowski, T., Nicklas, T., Uscanga, D., & Hanfling, M. (2011). The walking school bus and children's physical activity: A pilot cluster randomized controlled trial. *Pediatrics*, 128(3), e537–e544.

Miller, E., & Cushing, D. (2021). Theory-storming in the urban realm: Using nudge theory to inform the design of health-promoting places. *The Journal of Design Strategies*, 10(1), 112–121.

Nawrath, M., Kowarik, I., & Fischer, L. (2019). The influence of green streets on cycling behavior in European cities. *Landscape and Urban Planning*, 190, e103598.

Parikh, A., & Parikh, P. (2018). *Choice architecture: A new approach to behaviour, design and wellbeing*. Routledge.

Patuano, A., Shentova, R., & Aceska, A. (2022). Infrastructure and health: The salutogenic approach, interdisciplinarity and new challenges for planning and design. *International Journal of Managing Projects in Business*, ahead of print.

Portland Bureau of Transportation. (2019). *E-Scooter Findings Report*. Accessed from: https://www.portland.gov/sites/default/files/2020/pbot_e-scooter_report_final.pdf

Sweeney, J., Mee, K., McGuirk, P., & Ruming, K. J. (2018). Assembling placemaking: Making and remaking place in a regenerating city. *Cultural Geographies*, 25(4), 571–587.

Taylor, M. S., Wheeler, B. W., White, M. P., Economou, T., & Osborne, N. J. (2015). Research note: Urban street tree density and antidepressant prescription rates—A cross-sectional study in London, UK. *Landscape Urban Planning*, 135, 174–179.

World Health Organization. (2021). *Obesity and overweight*. Accessed from: https://www.who.int/news-room/fact-sheets/detail/obesity-and-overweight

8 Going places

Redesigning bikeways and multi-use trails to be more remarkable

Busy lifestyles mean we are often on the go, rushing from one place to the next, for work and play. Whether it is commuting to the office, picking up children from school, getting exercise on the weekends, or visiting friends and family, we need to get from point a to point b, and then, c, d, and e. There is a universal need to move around our communities efficiently and safely so that we can accomplish our daily activities. Although cars add convenience, relying predominately on them to get around can have well known repercussions – traffic congestion, increased carbon outputs, air and noise pollution, increased sedentary time, increased road rage and anxiety, accidents and unsafe conditions, and the expense of maintaining vehicles and transportation infrastructure. Alternative modes of transportation, including walking and cycling, which are active and environmentally friendly, require good bikeways and multi-use trails to make them realistic options.

Despite the environmental, physical, and economic benefits of walking and cycling, there are reasons we don't always do those activities. One key reason is that our urban areas are sometimes not designed appropriately. It is critical to minimise the additional effort required to use a bicycle instead of a car, or to walk instead of calling an uber. Efficiency is important. It is equally important to design a great experience. At a minimum, a bikeway or trail should follow a convenient route, afford good views, be shaded and well maintained, include easy access to amenities for food, drink, and rest, and be designed wide enough and smooth enough to afford a comfortable walk or ride. Going a step further, trail systems should be well-connected, fun and engaging, they should promote physical activity for all ages, and be built using sustainable materials. In short, they should be remarkable.

This chapter highlights innovative designs for bikeways and multi-use trails that include sustainable materials, roundabouts, and sophisticated infrastructure that can be implemented to afford walking and cycling. Redesigning bikeways and trails to be more functional and

DOI: 10.4324/9781003052746-10

motivating can enable people to make healthier choices, and are critical for sustainable, salutogenic, and playable urban environments.

The importance of walking and cycling

Walking is something many of us do every day. It is an activity in which people from all countries and walks of life (pun intended) participate. Young or old, rich or poor – we all walk. Models and celebrities walk fashion runways and popular music suggests we can *Walk the Line*, *Walk this Way*, *Walk on the Wild Side* and *Walk Like an Egyptian*. Walking 10,000 steps per day is a common goal for the everyday fitness enthusiast and the office worker participating in a global challenge, conveniently measured by the newest Garmin, Fitbit, and Apple trackers. Countless blog and Instagram posts detail how people have lost weight just by walking. And walking is often mentioned in research as the preferred physical activity within parks and open space (Duan et al., 2018).

Long distance walks are also popular. If you google famous walking trails around the world, you'll find anything from the *Camino de Santiago* (translated to the Way of St. James), a network of routes leading to the cathedral of Santiago de Compostela in north-western Spain; to the *Shikoku Pilgrimage* in Japan, which runs 1,400 km through 88 temples and 200 bangais along the coastline; to the *Cotswolds Way* in the United Kingdom, a 168 km path that takes you from Chipping Camden to Bath (Huang, 2022). The popularity of thru-walks, or long hikes, historically and in present day, indicate that people like to walk and can find it therapeutic, both for physical and mental health. Finding ways to encourage this more in urban environments on an everyday basis is the challenge.

Running and jogging, as opposed to walking or strolling, is more often done as a purposeful activity for physical fitness. That is unless you are running to catch a train or bus, or after a young child or dog who has gotten away. Running and jogging are also activities that are simple to undertake (although they require considerable effort), with minimal investment of personal resources. You only need to have a good pair of running shoes to go outside for a jog. And similar to walking, running can be done anywhere, but a dedicated multi-use trail is helpful to encourage it.

Cycling is also a popular way to get around or to get exercise. But bicycles have not always been welcome additions to public life. When the bicycle was first introduced in the early 1800s, it was prohibited from public squares and streets (Kosche, 2018). This history has ebbed and flowed. At one point the bicycle was ideal for urban transport, and at other times it was superseded by the automobile. Unlike walking and running, cycling requires equipment, and a larger dedicated space

128   Unremarkable spaces

for it to happen. Similarly, scootering, inline skating, skateboarding, and other wheeled activities require equipment to get started and a smooth ground plane.

Being able to walk and cycle are important for independent mobility. In many countries children once regularly rode through their neighbourhoods on bicycles. You might recall the classic bike ride in the California hills showing the 10-year old boy, Elliott, and his siblings to get the alien E.T. back to his spaceship. Children of course still ride bikes, but increased traffic and parental fears have potentially reduced this on neighbourhood streets in urban areas. In most countries, youth can't drive until they are 16 years or older, which means that if they cannot access the places they need or want to go by walking or cycling, they must rely on parents or caregivers, older siblings, and public transportation. This can put a strain on resources and limit their home range and independent mobility.

These activities (walking, running, scooting, etc.) are important for social engagement and can help bring people together, since most people can participate at low cost. Park runs and weekend races are popular social events drawing large crowds of like-minded people. And charity runs or fun runs can become large social and cultural activities, often accompanied with other activities for participating in and watching.

Designing spaces that encourage people to walk, run, cycle, skate, and scoot

Although these activities can be done anywhere, how we design spaces to encourage them matters. Research shows that designed environments can help afford these activities and make us more likely to do them. Spaces that afford walking and jogging, including sidewalks and bikeways (paved and unpaved), tend to be positively associated with physical activity (Giles-Corti et al., 2005; Kaczynski et al., 2008). And community parks that included walking loops saw 80% more people using them and they typically exerted higher levels of physical activity, than parks without walking loops (Cohen et al., 2017).

Dog walking is also a common activity in urban and suburban environments and accommodating dog walking can be a great way to encourage people to be active themselves. Research on dog walking and the impacts of dog ownership on walking behaviours suggests that dog walking can be one way to increase physical activity for some people. Based on data collected in the 2001 US National Household Travel Survey, researchers determined that in one day, 60% of dog walkers took two or more walks, 80% took at least one walk of 10 minutes or more, and 42% accumulated 30 minutes or more of walking (Ham & Epping, 2006). A meta-analysis of research on dog ownership found that approximately 60% of dog owners walked their dog for an average of 160 minutes per week and four times per week (Christian et al., 2013). Finding ways to encourage dog walking on multi-use trails is warranted.

Successful bikeways, walking paths, and multi-use trails not only need to function, but they need to be appealing aesthetically and contribute to the sense of place within their context. One such project that does this is the Nelson Street Cycleway in Auckland, New Zealand, which caters to both walkers and cyclists, and uses coloured pavement to create a distinctive pathway. The cycleway is noted for its magenta-coloured off-ramp, known as the Lightpath / Te Ara I Whiti, which includes interactive lights along one side. The project team worked with Maori artist Katz Maihi and iwi to include Maori designs and ensure the design captured the essence of the New Zealand context.[1] The Nelson Street Cycleway was featured in the Bicycle Architecture Biennale,[2] hosted by the Amsterdam-based global NGO BYCS to celebrate built environment innovations that facilitate bicycle travel. Although striking, the magenta-coloured pavement differs from other coloured pathways in that it does not incorporate standard and accepted colours, such as red, green, and blue (Autelitano & Giuliani, 2021).

Creating a significant separation between vehicles and bicycles and pedestrians is often paramount to safety. The Sands Street Cycle track in New York City, USA, for example, has been designed as a raised two-way bike track connecting the Manhattan Bridge and the Brooklyn Waterfront Greenway. According to the National Association of City Transportation Officials[3] the bikeway facilitates a safe and easy route onto the Manhattan Bridge (NACTO, n.d.). It also includes design features that are specific to its context and use. For example, it is 11 feet in width to easily allow snow-plowing and street-sweeping, and it includes an overhead signal and chevron markings to guide the transition onto the median bikeway for wayfinding purposes. Figure 8.1 shows an example of a multi-use trail with a separated pedestrian and bicycle path, with each divided into two directions.

In addition to the physical qualities of the pathway, the amenities require careful consideration. For example, you can walk a dog anywhere, but if the route also includes a water fountain, dog waste bags and trash bins, benches for rest, and trees for shade, it is that much more inviting. We discuss some of these elements, including benches and trash bins, in other chapters.

Gauging walk- and bike-ability

Whether it is the location, width, surface material, condition, adjacent land uses, or included facilities and amenities, the overall design of these

130 Unremarkable spaces

Figure 8.1 Multi-use trail with separated bicycle and pedestrian lanes.
Credit: Evonne Miller.

linear spaces to facilitate *going places* can have a significant impact on whether they are used and by whom. These are spaces that help create urban environments that are friendly, safe, and active. Unfortunately, the spaces set aside for pedestrians and bicycles are often considered secondary to streets. In relation to broken window theory, pathways and multi-use trails that are not pleasant experiences, send a message that it isn't where people should be. Interrupted or dead-end paths that don't reach a destination, and bikeways that merge with vehicular traffic can be intimidating, if not dangerous.

Similarly, sidewalks can often be hazardous to use (see Chapter 7 for a more extensive discussion of sidewalks, and the mobility opportunity and challenge posed by e-bikes). In some residential suburbs near Brisbane, Australia where we live, many side streets do not have sidewalks or pathways, or only have a sidewalk on one side of the street. If there are sidewalks, they often stop and start, either forcing people to walk on the grass or cross the street – not ideal for people who have difficulty walking or may be walking alongside children on bikes or scooters. Despite a general acceptance of walking and cycling in urban areas, there is still a need to gauge the walk- and bike-ability of a place to ensure it is designed to afford opportunities for these activities. Even when care has been taken to design a trail that accommodates different uses, mistakes can be made. Figure 8.2 shows examples of pathways that just end abruptly.

Figure 8.2 Examples of pathways that end abruptly from Brisbane, Australia.
Credit: Brent O'Neill; Debra Cushing.

Because of some of the challenges, walkability has become the focus for numerous researchers in urban design, land use planning, and landscape architecture over the last few decades (Blečić et al., 2020). Professional designers and community leaders are interested in analysing and evaluating walkability to inform policy, and subsequently improve the design of cities. Walkability measures often look at the interactions between people, urban space and the social context to give an indication about whether people are likely to walk there or not. Similarly, cycling assessments are also becoming more common in different cities and countries.

One example is the '3D layout', which describes the physical environment aspects of walkability, including density, diversity and design (Blečić et al., 2020; Cervero & Kockelman, 1997). The important environmental qualities of a walkable space were later described using the five Cs, which suggested that paths and trails needed to be connected, convenient, comfortable, convivial, and conspicuous (Gardner et al., 1996). Others have since introduced seven Cs, expanding the five Cs to include coexistence, which is the ability of pedestrians and other travel modes to coexist, and commitment, which is the accountability and responsibility of decision makers to create an environment conducive to walking (Sunarti et al., 2019).

Cycle-ability is also of interest, but perhaps not quite as common as walkability. Although bicycle enthusiasts and advocates tend to be much more passionate about creating great places to ride. In the book *Ride a Bike! Reclaim the City*, Becker et al. (2018) discuss key characteristics of urban spaces and cities that can impact the cycle-friendliness of a place. Highlighting cities such as Copenhagen, Oslo, Portland, New York City, and Barcelona, the authors discuss practices that we can learn from and be inspired by. Copenhagen, for example, is well known for its bicycle infrastructure and high population of residents commuting via bicycle. The city has a bicycle strategy titled, 'Good, Better, Best: The City of Copenhagen's Bicycle Strategy 2011–2025' (2011), which was created to help achieve, 'Copenhagen's goal of having a good city life and making Copenhagen CO_2 neutral by 2025' (p. 5).

In addition to Copenhagen, other large cities like Amsterdam, Utrecht, Bogota, and Vancouver are also well-known for their bike-friendly environments. Designing purposeful cues to demonstrate that spaces are maintained and safe, have amenities that are needed, and are designed with users in mind, can go a long way to encouraging people to use them. Factors such as safety and security, the presence of bicycle parking, protection from inclement weather, bicycle maintenance resources, and good connections between land uses are important. To help evaluate a city for bike-ability, Insurance tech start up, Coya, created The Bicycles Cities Index (Wired, 2019) which looked at: the percentage of bicycle users, safety, bicycle-related crime, road infrastructure, the number of stolen bicycles, cycling fatalities and accidents, the length of specialised cycling roads, road quality investments, and weather conditions including the average hours of sunshine, amount of rain and number of extreme weather days. In addition, the index considers the number of shared bicycles and rental stations, as well as the popularity of special cycling-related events such as No Car Day. These factors were compiled to determine the general bicycle-friendliness of a given city.

Other evaluation tools have taken a slightly different approach. To help categorise different types of bicycle infrastructure, researchers in Canada have introduced the Canadian Bikeway Comfort and Safety (Can-BICS) classification system to develop a common nomenclature about the safety and usability of bikeways, bicycle facilities, and roadways intended for cycling (Winters et al., 2020). The authors of the Can-BICS system acknowledge the importance of design for these spaces to ensure they maximise comfort and safety. The categories they developed are:

- *High-comfort bikeways*. These low-stress cycling facilities are comfortable for most people. Route types include cycle tracks alongside busy roads, local street bikeways and off-road bike paths.
- *Medium-comfort bikeways*. These low-to-medium stress cycling facilities are considered comfortable by some people. The off-road

infrastructure multi-use path fits within this category. Multi-use paths are shared with pedestrians and other active modes and can be located along a road or in an independent corridor.

- *Low-comfort bikeways*. These cycling facilities are high stress and comfortable for few people. The infrastructure type within this category is a painted bike lane, where people are cycling in a painted lane along busy roadways (p. 289).

Another classification system for bikeways is the *Urban Bikeway Design Guide* produced by the National Association of City Transportation Officials (NACTO).[4] This guide provides a typology of bicycle infrastructure commonly used in US communities, including: low-speed shared streets; bicycle boulevards; buffered and conventional bicycle lanes; protected bicycle lanes; and shared use and bicycle paths. One section in particular focuses on designing for all ages and abilities by creating cycle paths that are safe, comfortable, and equitable.

Why do bikeways and multi-use trails need to be remarkable?

There are many examples of well-designed bikeways and multi-use trails which are functional, enjoyable to use, and afford opportunities to exercise while being outside. But far too often, these spaces are not maintained and are considered secondary to traffic lanes and streets. People who are not as confident riding or walking alongside vehicle traffic may be less likely to use active transport if they need to compete with cars or drivers who are unaware or disrespectful of pedestrians and cyclists. When there are additional barriers, it becomes that much harder to convince people to use them. Designing them better cannot overcome all barriers, but it can go a long way to affording opportunities for more people.

Conflicts can arise between cars, bicycles, and pedestrians. Stories in the news often highlight a lack of respect from one party or the other to share the road. Injuries and death can result and create tension between the different users. Councils and transportation agencies ideally take responsible action and investigate the issues and how to make the environment better for both the cars and the bicycles. Solutions should be comprehensive and address the underlying cause of the conflict, rather than simply providing a band-aid. Meaningful and carefully planned alterations to the built environment can help address many of these challenges, including changes both simple and complex.

In addition to providing safe routes, redesigning bikeways and multi-use trails to nudge increased use is important if we want to counteract negative impacts of vehicle dependence and physical inactivity.

Unremarkable spaces

For most places, simply providing separated or designated trails and pathways is a start. Going further to focus on how these urban spaces are seen and experienced is critical to encouraging their effective and efficient use, as well as their enjoyment. Figure 8.3 shows a comparison of one bikeway that is functional for commuting but is poorly designed in terms of aesthetics and accommodating different users; with another that is not only functional but also supports an enjoyable

Figure 8.3 An efficient, but poorly designed bikeway on the left compared to a well-designed multi-use trail on the right.
Credits: Debra Cushing.

experience. Ironically, these are both along my daily bicycle commute to work near Brisbane, Australia.

In the following section, we describe two propositions: one to nudge healthy behaviours that include physical activity, and the other to nudge sustainability through the use of sustainable construction materials.

Proposition 1: Redesigning walking and cycling infrastructure to nudge physical activity

Creating a safe experience is an important consideration when designing bikeways and multi-use trails, especially if the intent is to increase physical activity and the amount of use. This often requires the careful separation from vehicle traffic and the recognition that pedestrians and cyclists should not be considered as secondary users. In some cases, this separation can be difficult and costly. But if done well, it can be remarkable.

A well-known example is the Hovenring in the Netherlands,[5] an iconic bicycle and pedestrian bridge that hovers over an intersection and marks the entrance to the cities of Eindhoven and Veldhoven. See Figure 8.4. Because the City of Eindhoven did not want a level crossing for cyclists that would require them to wait at the traffic light to continue their journey, they created a bicycle roundabout and that focused on the cyclist experience (Patowary, 2014). Designed by Dutch bridge specialist ipv Delft and completed in 2012, the circular bridge is made of steel suspended by cables attached to a pylon and is lit with LED lights at night.

Separating the cars from the cyclists and pedestrians was paramount to ensure safety and to provide a better experience. Lighting, gradients, and the vibrations of the cables were carefully considered to ensure the experience was enjoyable and that people would be encouraged to cycle or walk on the bridge and connecting trails (Becker et al., 2018). And connections were critical. The Hovenring is part of a 32 km long cycling route that connects important sites around the city. By creating a better and more convenient experience for pedestrians and cyclists, the infrastructure is nudging physical activity.

Since its completion, much has been written about the Hovenring and its iconic presence. Of note is the engineering, the collaboration between designers and engineers, the architectural quality and innovation, and the positioning at the entrance to the city. The bridge has become a city landmark and in 2014, it won the International Category of the Belgian Steel Construction Awards (ArcelorMittal, n.d.).

Although the Hovenring has received mostly praise and admiration for its innovative and striking design, it has also faced criticism. In particular, cyclists must accommodate the sloping gradient in order

136 Unremarkable spaces

Figure 8.4 The Hovenring roundabout in Eindhoven, the Netherlands.

Credit: European Cyclists' Federation (Flickr CC); European Cyclists' Federation (Flickr CC).

to rise above the vehicular traffic, rather than staying at the ground plane (Becker et al., 2018, p. 208). This could prove difficult for some cyclists who are not as fit, and for some people it could be perceived as an insurmountable barrier. However, it should be noted that in an attempt to minimise the incline of the cycleway, the roadway beneath was lowered by 1.5 m (ArcelorMittal, n.d.).

Proposition 2: Nudging sustainability by building trails with sustainable materials

By their nature, bikeways and multi-use paths are more sustainable than streets since they enable eco-friendly transportation and require fewer construction resources due to their reduced width and load requirements. However, concrete is the standard surface material for creating smooth, consistent surfaces, despite the high levels of carbon emissions it produces. Estimates suggest concrete is responsible for at least 8% of total carbon emissions produced by humans world-wide (Ellis et al., 2019).

Lighting along pathways is also critical for safety and night-time use, but it also requires considerable energy costs and can be a huge source of carbon emissions. For example, in Australia, street lighting is the single largest source of carbon emissions for local government, with lighting in some areas as high as 60% of total emissions (Energyrating.gov.au)! And although a switch to LED (light emitting diodes) lighting options may improve the carbon footprint, it may also cause other significant issues. Some research suggests that LED lighting increases light pollution, will more significantly impact nocturnal wildlife activity in urban areas, and may suppress the production of melatonin in humans and other animals (Mohameed, 2022).

One way to reduce the need for overhead path lighting is to use innovative materials. Light-emitting concrete, described as self-luminous or glow-in-the-dark, could be an option. For this example, we go back to the City of Eindhoven for a unique use of light-emitting concrete to create an artistic and sustainable pathway. In 2014, Dutch designer Daan Roosegaarde created 1,970 feet of pathway reminiscent of van Gogh's The Starry Night (Cross, 2019). It is described as 'solar-powered techno-poetry evoking the familiar swirls of *Starry Night*' (Gilburne, 2014). The effect is created by thousands of luminescent blue-green rocks wrapped in a photo-sensitive coating and embedded in concrete.

These types of materials can be created in multiple ways, including mixing luminous materials, such as fluorescent aggregates and powders, into the concrete mixture; or coating the concrete surface with a glow-in-the-dark sealant material (Han et al., 2017). In the town of Lidzbark Warmiński in the northern part of Poland, you can also find a glow in the dark bike path powered by the sun (Cross, 2019). A prototype of 330 feet long bicycle path absorbs solar radiation during the day and emits fluorescent light in the dark has been built.[6] The 6-foot wide path cost approximately $31,000 to build (Metcalf, 2016). The material uses phosphors to glow blue for about 10 hours, increasing the level of safety during night-time riding.

Conclusion

Much of the research literature and policy initiatives recommend ways that cities need to encourage walking and cycling on a large scale. They often mention creating connections between environments in which we live, work, and play. These activities are not only important for increasing physical activity rates and improving overall health and well-being, they have social and cultural implications that make them vital in our urban environments. In this chapter, we have discussed just a sampling of innovative design ideas we can look to for inspiration to create more remarkable bikeways and multi-use trails and improve our experiences of our urban environments.

Notes

1 For more information about the Nelson Street Cycleway see https://www.nzta.govt.nz/projects/nelson-street-cycleway/
2 Read more about the bicycle biennale at https://bycs.org/the-bicycle-architecture-biennale/.
3 See https://nacto.org/case-study/sands-street-two-way-protected-cycle-track-brooklyn-ny/
4 For the NACTO Design Guide see https://nacto.org/publication/urban-bikeway-design-guide/.
5 For more information on the Hovenring, see https://ipvdelft.com/projects/hovenring/.
6 Watch a video showing the glow-in-the-dark path at https://youtu.be/eu38SHyj-XY.

References

ArcelorMittal Europe Communications. (n.d.). *Fabric of life: Hovenring increases safety for vulnerable road users.* Downloaded 3 October 2022 from https://europe.arcelormittal.com/fol_hovenring

Autelitano, F., & Giuliani, F. (2021). Colored bicycle lanes and intersection treatments: International overview and best practices. *Journal of Traffic and Transportation Engineering, 8*(3), 399–420.

Becker, A., Lampe, S., Negussie, L., & Cachola Schomal, P. (2018). *Ride a bike!: Reclaim the City.* Walter de Gruyter GmbH.

Blečić, I., Congiu, T., Fancello, G., & Trunfio, G. (2020). Planning and design support tools for walkability: A guide for urban analysts. *Sustainability, 12,* 4405.

Cervero, R., & Kockelman, K. (1997). Travel demand and the 3Ds: Density, diversity, and design. *Transportation Research Part D: Transport and Environment, 2*(3), 199–219.

Christian, H., Westgarth, C., Bauman, A., Richards, E., Rhodes, R., Evenson, K., Mayer, J., & Thorpe, R. (2013). Dog ownership and physical activity: A review of the evidence. *Journal of Physical Activity and Health, 10*(5), 750–759.

City of Copenhagen, Technical and Environmental Administration. (2011). Downloaded 4 August 2022 from file:///Users/cushingd/Downloads/bicycle-strategi-2011-2025-_823%20(1).pdf

Cohen, D, Han, B., Evenson, K., Nagel, C., McKenzie, T., Marsh, T., Williamson, S., Harnik, P. (2017). The prevalence and use of walking loops in neighborhood parks: A national study. *Environmental Health Perspectives*, 125(2), 170–174.

Cross, D. (2019). *A sun-powered bicycle path glows in the dark in Poland* (15 April, 2019). Downloaded 4 August 2022 from https://www.sustainability-times.com/clean-cities/a-sun-powered-bicycle-path-glows-in-the-dark-in-poland/#:~:text=In%20the%20town%20of%20Lidzbark, for%20people%20on%20their%20bicycles

Duan, Y., Wagner, P., Zhang, R., Wulff, H., & Brehm, W. (2018). Physical activity areas in urban parks and their use by the elderly from two cities in China and Germany. *Landscape and Urban Planning*, 178, 261–269.

Ellis, L., Badel, A., Chiang, M., Park, R., & Chiang, Y. (2019). Toward electrochemical synthesis of cement—An electrolyzer-based process for decarbonating $CaCO_3$ while producing useful gas streams. *Proceedings of the National Academy of Sciences of the United States of America*, 117(23), 12584–12591.

Energyrating.gov.au. (2020). *Street and public lighting.* Downloaded 12 August 2022 from https://www.energyrating.gov.au/products/street-and-public-lighting#toc1

Gardner, K., Johnson, T., Buchan, K. & Pharaoh, T. (1996). Developing a pedestrian strategy for London. In: *ETC Proceedings, London.* http://www.etcproceedings.org/paper/developing-a-pedestrian-strategy-for-london

Gilburne, M. (October 31, 2014). *Van Gogh's Starry Night re-created in an innovative bike path: An innovative solar bike path pays homage to Van Gogh's Starry Night.* Downloaded 3 October 2022 from https://www.architecturaldigest.com/story/van-gogh-bike-path

Giles-Corti, B., Broomhall, M., Knuiman, M., Collins, C., Douglas, K., Ng, K., Lange, A., & Donovan, R. (2005). Increasing walking: How important is distance to, attractiveness, and size of public open space? *American Journal of Preventive Medicine*, 28(2), 169–176.

Ham, S. A., & Epping, J. (2006). Dog walking and physical activity in the United States. *Preventing Chronic Disease.* http://www.cdc.gov/pcd/issues/2006/apr/05_0106.htm

Han, B., Zhang, L., & Ou, J. (2017). Light-emitting concrete. In *Smart and multifunctional concrete toward sustainable infrastructures.* Springer. https://doi.org/10.1007/978-981-10-4349-9_16

Huang, N. (2022). *10 of the most famous walking trails in the world* (3 March 2022). Downloaded 4 August 2022 from https://www.wildjunket.com/most-famous-walking-trails-in-the-world/

Kaczynski, A., Potwarka, L., & Saelens, B. (2008). Association of park size, distance, and features with PA in neighborhood parks. *American Journal of Public Health*, 98(8), 1451–1456.

Kosche, T. (2018). A 200-year Battle for position: The bicycle in urban transport. In A. Becker, S. Lampe, L. Negussie, & P. C. Schmal (Eds.), *Ride a bike!: Reclaim the city* (pp. 16–21). Birkhäuser Verlag GmbH.

Metcalf, J. (2016). Poland tests a self-sufficient, glow-in-the-dark bike path. *Bloomberg.* Downloaded 3 October 2022 from https://www.bloomberg.com/news/articles/2016-10-11/a-glowing-bike-path-that-s-charged-by-the-sun-in-poland.

Mohameed, W. (2022). Increase in LED Lighting 'risks harming human and animal health'. *The Guardian.* Downloaded 3 October 2022 from https://www.theguardian.com/environment/2022/sep/14/increase-in-led-lighting-risks-harming-human-and-animal-health.

140 Unremarkable spaces

NACTO (National Association of City Transportation Officials). (n.d.). *Sands street bicycle path and Greenstreet, New York City, NY.* Downloaded 4 October 2022 from https://nacto.org/case-study/sands-street-two-way-protected-cycle-track-brooklyn-ny/

Patowary, K. (2014). Hovenring, the floating circular cycle bridge in Eindhoven. *Amusing Planet website.* Downloaded 4 October 2022 from https://www.amusingplanet.com/2014/01/hovenring-floating-circular-cycle.html

Sunarti, E. T., Tribhuwaneswari, A., Rachmalisa, O., & Kurniasanti, R. (2019). Urban environmental quality and human well-being assessment: Towards walkable neighborhood (a case study of Dr. Soetomo Hospital, Surabaya). In T. Kerr, B. Ndimande, J. Van der Putten, D. F. Johnson-Mardones, D. Arimbi, & Y. Amalia (Eds.), *Urban studies: Border and mobility.* Taylor & Francis Group.

Winters, M., Zanotto, M., & Butler, G. (2020). The Canadian bikeway comfort and safety (Can-BICS) classification system: A common naming convention for cycling infrastructure. *Health Promotion Chronic Disease Prevention in Canada*, 40(9):288–293.

Wired. (2019). *The 20 most bike-friendly cities on the planet, ranked: The 2019 Copenhagenize Index ranks the world's urban hubs on how much they're doing to promote life on two wheels.* Downloaded 2 October 2022 from https://www.coya.com/bike/index-2019

9 Staying put

Redesigning parking lots to be remarkable

Have you purchased your last car? Based on an evaluation of market, consumer, and regulatory dynamics, and technology-driven disruption, researchers are predicting urban transportation systems are on the brink of radical change. Instead of private cars, our transport future is likely to be on-demand autonomous electric vehicles: these driverless shared cars are envisioned to alleviate traffic congestion, improve road safety, reduce environmental impacts, and enhance mobility for the young, old, and people with disabilities (Fagnant & Kockelman, 2015; RethinkX, 2017). This predicted emergence of autonomous vehicles will significantly alter transport systems – including the design, provision, and usage of the public space where many cars are stored when not in use: parking lots.

While we stand on the verge of a car-less future, right now parking spaces and lots – whether roadside, off-street, open-air, or enclosed parking buildings – remain one of the most unremarkable and utilitarian spaces in our cities. And there are a lot more of them then you may realise. In the United States, there are a billion parking spots: eight spots for every car, with parking estimated to take up nearly a third of land area in American cities (Ben-Joseph, 2012). Typically sized around 2.5 m (7.5–9 feet) in width and 5.4 m (10–20 feet) in length, parking lot regulations tend to focus on the minimum or maximum number of parking spaces, along with issues of size, entry, and egress – but never the actual design of the lot, which rarely varies. As Eran Ben-Joseph (2012) reminds us in his engaging book, *Rethinking a lot*[1]:

> One look at a typical parking lot raises many questions. Can parking lots be designed in a more attractive and aesthetically pleasing way? Can environmental considerations be addressed and adverse effects mitigated? Can parking lots provide more than car storage? Can they be integrated into our built environment - not only as a practical necessity, but also as something elegant and enjoyable? What

DOI: 10.4324/9781003052746-11

can we learn from studying usage behaviour and manipulation of lots by unlikely users such as kids, food vendors, theatre companies, and sports fans? And finally, are there any great parking lots that can inspire alternatives?

(2012, p. xii)

In this chapter, we argue that the design and use of parking lots does not need to be formulaic and utilitarian but can in fact nudge human and planetary health. From community sites for opera, concerts, markets, play, exercise, and social connection, to purposefully sustainable landscapes, materials and structures that celebrate nature, conserve water, or generate energy, our proposition is that parking lots have the potential to transition from unremarkable spaces to remarkable community assets. Too often, however, parking lot design tends to focus on 'pedestrian safety, ease of circulation, and standard dimensions... [not] aesthetics or the integration of the parking lot with its immediate surroundings' (Trautvetter, 2018, p. 213). This chapter, drawing on the key lens of sustainable, salutogenic and playable design, encourages us to think differently and creatively about the design of parking lots.

Proposition 1: Nudging environmental sustainability through eco-friendly parking lots

We start by thinking how the thoughtful design of parking lots, along with the rest of our urban environment, might nudge environmental sustainability. Alongside the United Nations 17 Sustainable Development Goals (SDG) which provide invaluable higher-level goals in terms of how we might achieve sustainable cities and communities, the *C40 Cities* global network of nearly 100 mayors of diverse and world-leading cities (including Milan, Houston, Auckland, Oslo, Paris, and Mexico City) are collaborating to take urgent action on the climate crisis – and as we will see, an important part of their vision includes redesigning and reclaiming parking lots!

C40 Cities members earn their membership through action: to join, mayors must have developed city-level specific commitments and actions on climate change, which includes transport strategies for active, climate, and people-friendly streets, rather than prioritising cars and parking lots. Through mutual learning, cross-boundary collaboration, new discourses, networks and best-practice policy, and initiative sharing, C40 supports member cities to implement, scale-up, leverage, and experiment creatively with climate projects from 'built environment change, new citizen practices, policy change, infrastructural change and new technology' (Nguyen et al., 2020, p. 1). And, in the post-pandemic phase, the C40 group is advocating for a 'green and just' recovery agenda – to build back better with an intentional focus on climate, social, and economic justice (C40, 2022).

As part of a broader sustainability strategy, many C40 members have transformed parking lots in their cities. As part of their quest to become the world's first carbon neutral capital by 2025, C40 member city Copenhagen has reduced the number of parking lots and replaced them with natural urban infrastructure (shrubs, bushes, trees) with the canopies creating shade that reduces the urban heat island effect while also enhancing air quality and circulation. As part of its C40 commitment, Paris recently pledged to remove half (70,000) of its 140,000 on-street-car parking spaces to (1) create more public spaces for Parisians, who often live in cramped flats and (2) add green urban infrastructure, to help mitigate the impacts of climate change and make the air more breathable. Residents get to decide what will replace the 10 square metre parking places, with options including trees and plants, vegetable allotments, food composting, children's playgrounds, and bicycle lock-up areas.[2]

Greening our urban landscape: from asphalt to aesthetically and environmentally friendly

To help mitigate the impacts of climate change, cities are increasingly integrating sustainable nature-based solutions, urban greening, and urban green infrastructure to create more multi-functional natural 'green-blue' (nature and water) environments in dense city spaces. A large body of research has shown that nature improves our urban micro-climate: from street trees, vegetated urban spaces, gardens, parks, waterways, habitat corridors and nature reserves, living walls, and green roofs, the purposeful integration of nature is a key strategy for cooling our built environment, treating air and water, and increasing habitat for biodiversity (Kindermann et al., 2021).

Reclaiming parking lots, from smaller on street parking to larger closed and open-air spaces, is a key strategy for re-integrating nature into our urban environments. Traditional parking lots are typically acres of asphalt and non-permeable concrete surfaces; however, many could be easily redesigned to be urban green infrastructure – to become environmentally friendly, spatially effective, and aesthetically pleasing 'fields' of nature. Landscape architect Trautvetter (2018) has a vision of concrete parking lots being turned into 'fields' of nature, explaining that 'planting the entire lot would decrease the heat island effect, provide corridors for wildlife, and minimize stormwater runoff during slow retail months, while being easily mowed down during periods of high traffic' (p. 217), while also turning the parking experience into an adventure: 'which areas will be wildflowers and grasses? Which will be mowed and accessible?' (p. 219).

144 Unremarkable spaces

Mitigating the heat island and stormwater management

Redesigning parking lots also addresses the heat island effect, which is where the over-abundance of impervious urban structures (pavements, buildings, roads, and parking lots) that absorb, retain, and re-emit the sun's heat much more than natural landscapes (grass, trees, forests, water) means urbanised areas experience higher temperatures than nearby rural areas. For example, the dark pavements of single storey open-air parking lots are exposed to direct solar radiation all day, which aggravates surface and air temperatures. Additionally, the hard surfaces of streets and parking lots are also the main contributor to excess stormwater runoff: the hard ground cannot absorb the water from rain or snowstorms, which flows over hard surfaces (streets, parking lots, and roofs) collecting pollutants before entering a storm drain or water body (read more about the urban heat island effect in Chapter 5).

Designing parking lots to be environmentally friendly and adding vegetation cover (trees, grass, and shrubs) significantly mitigates the heat island affect and improves stormwater management. Modelling data from Japan, of planting grass on the surface or covering the lot with 30% trees and 70% grass, showed that greening parking lots could reduce the land surface temperature in summer by 7.4–9.2°C, respectively. Of course, as the authors acknowledged, the exact shading and cooling potential of a green parking lot varies depending on vegetation species, growth, spatial arrangement, tree size and shading, maintenance, and irrigation (Onishi et al., 2010).

As well as adding vegetation in as many forms as feasible, green parking lots also often replace hard impervious surfaces (a barrier to the normal ecological life cycle of water) with permeable, porous pavers (gravel, pebbles, brick, wood mulch, cobblestones, natural stone, grass paving blocks) that enable natural drainage and the filtering and removal of sediments and pollutants. These water efficient choices reduce the volume and rate of stormwater runoff, which helps to prevent flooding and improve the water quality of our streams and rivers.

In her book, *Wild by Design*, Margie Ruddick (2016) provides a wonderful example of how thoughtful consideration of paver design can contribute, significantly, to the creation and experience of place. Queens Plaza, the gateway to Long Island City from Manhattan, spans eight city blocks and utilises a constructed wetland and subsurface filtration systems to prevent over 20 million gallons of stormwater from entering the city's sewers. Artist Michael Singer's studio designed interlocking and modular permeable pavers that provide a safe walling surface and direct stormwater to the plantings – while also featuring sculptural details. These permeable pavers show graphic scoring relating to the site's industrial history, with this grooved medium serving as (1) water conveyance, directing water from the path to the wetland; (2) art object; and (3) enabling mosses and herbs to grow, over time, in the cracks (Ruddick, 2016).

While sculptural details permeable pavers remain rare, bioswales are aesthetically pleasing natural stormwater management system that is an increasingly popular alternative to concrete gutters and storm sewers. Narrow, long, and shallow and gently sloping grass or vegetated channels which capture and naturally treats stormwater as it moves downstream, bioswales are contemporary best practice rainwater/stormwater management.[3] Bioswales transform streets, car parks and parking lots into places for nature that benefits human and planetary health.

Designing for extreme weather events

Redesigning urban spaces such as parking lots with urban microclimate, thermal comfort and stormwater management in mind is an important strategy for enhancing urban climate adaptation and mitigating the impacts of extreme weather events (e.g. heatwaves, drought, flooding). Indeed, as we are writing this chapter in February 2022, heavy torrential rains and a 'rain bomb' hit our state of Queensland in Australia, resulting in significant flash flooding and the wettest three-day period in the capital city of Brisbane since weather records began in 1840: 24.1 inches (611.6 mm) of rain fell in three days, from Friday morning to Sunday evening. Seven people died and schools were closed, as homes, streets and parks were inundated with flood water (Jordan, 2022). The rain and waters continued to the neighbouring state, New South Wales, where an unprecedented 14.4 metre high flood killed four people and destroyed thousands of homes in the riverside regional town of Lismore.

Although a detailed discussion of urban design for flood-mitigation is beyond the scope of this chapter, increasing climate extremes and variability means we must intentionally redesign public parks and green parking lots for climate change preparedness and response – for example, as 'sponges' to reduce the impact of flash flooding in dense urban areas (Graça et al., 2022; Hamidi et al., 2021). The Edwards Gardens/Toronto Botanical Garden Sustainable Parking Lot in Ontario, Canada is a good example of applying sustainable design principles to retrofit a 15,045 m^2 parking lot located beside a creek.

In 2012, landscape designers Schollen and Company Inc transformed this space into a green parking lot: a 880 m^2 network of stormwater bioswales was installed in traffic islands, alongside permeable pavers on parking spaces and walkways, the enhancement of a tree canopy

146 **Unremarkable spaces**

and extensive native plantings (including replacing lawn with native vegetation), with a significant focus on conserving and recusing existing materials during construction – the original fencing was restored and incorporated into the design and the asphalt surf of the existing parking lot was recycled into sub-base material for the green parking lot (Sustainable Technologies Evaluation Program, 2016).

The walls and roofs of parking lots: from green roofs, vertical urban farms to solar canopies

The walls and roofs of parking lots can also be more sustainable, facilitating climate adaptation, food accessibility, and economic inclusivity. Despite logistical challenges with design, installation, construction, and operation, a small but growing number of parking lots feature green roofs and rooftop (vertical) fruit and vegetable farms. Green roofs and walls are increasing commonplace in our built environment. Alongside their obvious environmental benefits of building cooling and insulation (therefore lowering energy consumption), living green roofs and walls also absorb sound to make cities quieter.

Chicago's Millennium Park is one of the largest green roofs in the world and is constructed on top of a railroad yard and large parking garages. In downtown Detroit, Michigan the roof of the nine-story, 1,825-space parking garage at Blue Cross Blue Shield's headquarters is green – and a sports area, featuring a 160 m jogging track made of recycled rubber paving for employee walking.[4] Completed in November 2006, this parking garage was the first LEED® certified parking structure, recycling rain and irrigation water to water the landscaping. More recently, in 2015 in Australia, a $23.3 million four storey car park was built on Griffith University's Gold Coast campus. Featuring green walls, solar panels, and a highly visible wind turbine, this 1,150 vehicle car park provides enough power to run the car park and offset other nearby buildings, as well as four native bee boxes and 10 microbat boxes.

Unused large-scale asphalt parking lots and their roofs are also being turned into urban farms, with such hyper-local food production providing more efficient food supply chains, food security, and food equity, while simultaneously addressing economic, social, and environmental sustainability considerations (Harada & Whitlow, 2020). In the United States, for example, social enterprise Vertical Harvest, which operates under an inclusive employment model focused on individuals with physical and/or intellectual disabilities, creates urban farms in underutilised space in underserved urban neighbourhoods. Vertical Harvest's most recent project, which began construction in April 2022, is a public private partnership in Westbrook, Maine (part of Greater Portland) to re-develop the Mechanic Street public parking lot into a farm that will produce 1 million pounds of produce annually. In Paris, agricultural start-up Cycloponics grows mushrooms in a 9,000 m² disused multistorey parking facility underneath a social housing complex, while in Vancouver, Alterrus Systems has created the first commercial farming operation in North America on the roof of a busy urban parking lot.

As well as generating food, parking lots can be designed to generate energy – with speed bumps able to capture and harness the 'up and down' vibration and kinetic energy generated by vehicles as they are driving over (Li et al., 2022). In the United Kingdom, Sainsbury's – which has pledged to be carbon neutral by 2040 – has installed these 'kinetic road plates' in the car park of Gloucester store, with the power generated by vehicles passing over them (30 kW of green energy/hour) said to be enough to run the cash registers.

More significant in terms of energy generation are solar farms and solar canopies: elevated structures that sit over land already being used for something else. While most solar farms are located on undeveloped rural land, as it is cheaper to develop, solar canopies are increasingly being added to large parking lots across the globe. Figure 9.1 shows an example of a parking lot solar canopy – at the Google corporate headquarters. Co-locating solar canopies on large, underutilised parking lots is a sensible choice, as it: uses existing land, shades cars, reduces energy costs, and the urban heat island effect, while producing green electricity for local communities. A recent American study used

Figure 9.1 Example of a parking lot solar canopy, at Google corporate headquarters.
Credit: Steve Proehl Getty Images #21642486 (royalty-free).

geo-spatial analysis to explore the viability of adding solar canopies to all large parking lots (100+ spaces) in Connecticut. Rudge (2021) found that solar canopies sited across 8,416 suitable locations had the potential to produce a third (37%; 9,042 gigawatt-hours) of the state's current electricity consumption and would also foster social equity, as such community solar projects help to decentralise the energy system.

Parking lots are obvious sites for local solar canopies, as our society continues to transition away from fossil fuel plants which produce substantial greenhouse gases and local air pollution. There are a growing number of exemplar solar canopy projects. In 2020, the Washington Metropolitan Area Transit Authority contracted the building of its first solar canopies at four rail station parking lots (a US$50 project with a projected capacity of 12.8 megawatts; Pickerel, 2020), as did Disneyland Paris. To be completed in 2023, the 17 hectares (42 acres) of solar canopies in Disneyland Paris parking lots will use 67,500 solar panels to produce 31 gigawatt-hours per year, generating 17% of the resorts power and reducing greenhouse gas emissions by 750 tons of carbon dioxide per year. As well as producing renewable clean energy, the solar canopies will provide shade from rain, snow, and sunlight, with a sense of fun built into the design: at night, the shape of a Mickey Mouse head will be illuminated (Walt Disney Company, 2020).

Proposition 2: Nudging health by turning parking lots into salutogenic spaces

The design, use and number of parking lots can also enhance citizens' health and well-being, with many cities across the globe replacing parking with places for the public to interact, exercise and be in nature. Parking lots are perfect places for physically active games, such as basketball, soccer, hopscotch, tennis, and street hockey (Ben-Joseph, 2012), with their surface and walls providing a wonderful public place for sport and exercise.

Streets and parking lots: closed to traffic, open to physical activity – Ciclovía

Alongside PARKing Day, discussed in detail in Chapter 7, perhaps the most well-known example of temporarily turning streets and parking lots into places for people is seen in the capital city of Colombia, Bogotá: to promote urban biking, socialising, playing and physical exercise, every Sunday from 7 am to 2 pm, 120 kilometres (70 miles) of Bogotá streets are closed to cars, creating inclusive spaces for people to interact.

Widely praised as an innovative example of transformative urban experimentation (Montero, 2017), the first 'Ciclovía' was held in

1974, with a million people now participating each week. Globally, there are 497 Ciclovía programmes in 27 countries – and the research shows that these programmes promote physical activity and healthy lifestyles for adults and children (Sarmiento et al., 2017; Triana et al., 2019), while also enhancing quality of life and having a positive environmental impact on air pollution and quality.

Inspired by Ciclovía, many cities now hold similar open street programmes that encourage healthy lifestyles and provide safe spaces for traffic-free cycling, skating, walking, dancing, and connecting. The evaluation of an open street Ciclovía event in Los Angeles (CicLAvia) in 2014 shows the impact: using intercept surveys and 14 surveillance cameras, the between 37,700 and 53,950 active participants generated 176,500 to 263,000 MET (metabolic equivalent) hours of energy expenditure, at an estimate cost to the tax payers of US\$1.29 to US\$1.91 per MET-hour. Interestingly over a third (37%) had never previously participated in CicLAvia – and most (45%) said if they were not there, they would have been sedentary (Cohen et al., 2016).

Globally, streets and parking lots are increasingly being transformed into places and spaces for walking and playing. While the terminology differs, from home zones in the United Kingdom, the *woonerf* in the Netherlands and the more recent Living Streets Experiment across multiple European cities (see Gysels, 2020), the notion of shared and carless streets is gaining international traction. In Ghent, for example, over 100 'Living Streets' where created – created as a transition experiment, residents reimagined what their neighbourhood could look like, taking control of their street as a living laboratory to transform them as they wished for several months. Interestingly, at a very practical level, the biggest challenge was finding solutions for parking: 'where to park, how can we still load and unload, parking for visitors, parking for nurses and doctors at home for those who are depending on this' (Gysels, 2020, pp. 271–272). Successfully activating local streets for people requires the consideration and development of new parking options: from more sustainable mobility options (e-bikes, car sharing) to providing dedicated parking for nurses and doctor visits and the identification of new communal parking spaces in the neighbourhood.

Whether it is 'living' streets, Ciclovía or PARKing Days, these street experiments are powerful examples of tactical urbanism: low-cost temporary changes to the urban built environment that create space for people to view and use streets (and parking lots) differently. As sustaining such urban transformations and ensuring that they serve as critical catalysts of *system-wide transformations* is not easy, Bertolini (2020) has outlined five key characteristics that will help ensure street experiments trigger a longer-term change trajectory. Drawing

150   **Unremarkable spaces**

on Roorda et al.'s (2014) five defining characteristics of transition experiments, Bertolini (2020) argues that street experiments must be:

- *Radical:* Are the practices foregrounded by the experiment fundamentally different from dominant practices?
- *Challenge driven:* Is the experiment a step towards a potentially long-term change pathway to address a societal challenge?
- *Feasible:* Is it possible to realise the experiment in the short term and with readily available resources?
- *Strategic:* Can the experiment generate lessons about how to reach the envisioned fundamental changes? Can the agents needed for such changes access these lessons?
- *Communicative/mobilising:* Can news about the experiment reach and possibly mobilise the broader public?

Redesigning parking lots post-pandemic

The COVID-19 pandemic – which kept most people at home and accessing local environments more – has also impacted the design and use of public spaces and parking lots As well as seeing greater numbers of people exercising in local streets (see Chapter 7), as personal vehicles remained parked at home, the lack of cars on roads reduced pollution and congestion, making the space more accessible. From Melbourne to Milan, city planners across the globe took the opportunity to quickly turn car parks and roads for cars, temporarily and permanently, into cycle lanes, walkways, and public space that enabled socially distanced exercise and commuting (see Chapters 7 and 8). Several cities have also pledged to remove car parks to create space for people, nature, exercise, and play. In Amsterdam, where 65% of everyday commuting trips are made via bike, the Greens party is removing 10,000 parking spaces by 2025 (1,500 parking spaces a year[5]) from the city centre, replacing them with public green and play spaces, co-designed with residents.

How space is used also sends an implicit message about what our society values. As COVID-19 closed many gyms, the popularity of outdoor workouts in unusual locations has soared. As well as the more traditional park locations, growing numbers of personal trainers are hosting 'curbside' and 'parking lot' workouts, turning these urban public places into places for exercise – usually simpler aerobic movement and body weight exercise, but occasionally also portable equipment (hand weights, skipping ropes) for strength, fitness, and coordination. From shuttle runs to squats, parking lot[6] and street workouts facilitate health: thus, while permanent outdoor fitness stations are increasingly commonplace in parks, creating an exercise trail/walking circuit that explicitly includes activities in parking lots is an unusual idea that might further promote health.

Of course, while parking lots can be used for exercise, we also acknowledge that large open-air parking lots often also serve as homes for the homeless (Wehman-Brown, 2016). As the number of homeless people living on the streets and in their cars is growing, so too are the number of global 'safe parking' programmes, which opens parking lots at night for homeless people who live in their vehicles. While the logistics varies, these programmes provide a safe and legal place for people to sleep in their vehicle in a parking lot; some offer security guards and bathrooms, clothes, and meals, as well as access to case management, social and health support services (Holder, 2019).

In Australia, the not-for-profit Beddown[7] is experimenting with a novel approach: turning *covered* indoor city centre parking lots (vacant and unused overnight) into temporary accommodation by physically installing beds (with sheets, blankets, and pillows) into the parking lot. In Britain, to provide disadvantaged young people with homes, 11 affordable, eco-friendly modular pods have been installed on stilts above the St. George carpark in Bristol – the Zedpod. As autonomous vehicles will likely reduce the need for streets and parking, some authors are arguing that these spaces be turned into housing (see Millard-Ball, 2021), with the pod solution one out of the box idea already being trailed to address the growing social housing crisis.

Proposition 3: Nudging play through the design of parking lots and buildings

Finally, parking lots provide important spaces for play. From screening movies, hosting music bands, pop-up food trucks, fairs and events, and the opera, to sites of fresh food and flea markets, and places where children learn to ride their bikes and teens learn to dive their first car, parking lots can be sites of fun, play and adventure. Like streets, when designed and used with intention parking lots can be great places for people to gather, interact, connect, and play. Fortunately, designers are increasingly challenging the mono-functional and conventional design and use of parking lots and designing these spaces to also be attractive public spaces that facilitate fun.

The unconventional design of the roof of parking buildings can facilitate play, as we see in Figures 9.2–9.4. In Copenhagen, Denmark, the recent *rooftop* refurbishment of an eight-story parking building into an 'urban living space' with sports and play equipment provides much inspiration for turning parking buildings into sites of play.

Designed by JAJA Architects, this project in the neighbourhood of Nordhavnen – entitled Parking House + Konditaget Lüders (aka

152   Unremarkable spaces

Figure 9.2 Rooftop public space and harbour views at Parking House + Konditaget Lüders.
Credit: Rasmus Hjortshøj/Coast Studio for JAJA Architects.

Figure 9.3 Roof top playground, running track and exercise at Parking House + Konditaget Lüders.
Credit: Rasmus Hjortshøj/Coast Studio for JAJA Architects.

Figure 9.4 Exterior stairs and frieze of Parking House + Konditaget Lüders.
Credit: Rasmus Hjortshøj/Coast Studio for JAJA Architects.

'PARK "N" PLAY') won the 2020 Danish Design Award in the 'Liveable Cities' category. The jury praised how this playable design solution as 'the first time we have seen a parking house come alive. The living roof has been incorporated into the building in a very intelligent way, allowing people to run and play, while giving them access to a view... we have seen the use of rooftops for leisure before – e.g. for private tennis courts and pools – but with its public access, this solution has a democratic appeal'. In a video[8] reflecting on the design process, co-founders of JAJA Architects Kathrin Susanna Gimmel and Jan Yoshiyuki Tanaka, explain the joy of designing a parking garage as a public space, purposely creating space for people, and how they made a conscious decision to make the rooftop playable with the space purposely red, to reflect the red brick heritage of the surroundings.

Alongside the rooftop playground, there are several other notable design decisions that help make this parking building unremarkable. A series of green planters hang along the façade of the building to provide both greenery and a sense of scale which celebrates rather than hides the parking building. The exterior stairs are a continuous red thread that leads people up from street, past the green façade to the public space and playground on the rooftop, while the frieze is educational and depicts historic tales (significant buildings, structures, activities) from the harbour that have shaped the history of Nordhavnen.

In their thought-provoking book, Jensen and Lanng (2017) argue that – given our mobile urban lifestyles – the location and function of parking lots mean they could play a much more significant role in daily life, as a critical place of contact and social interactions. More than simply a place for parking cars, a parking lot is a site of 'ambiguous mobility... of rest, activity, meeting, experience and consumption' (p. 115). Designed thoughtfully, as in the example from JAJA Architects have, parking lots can indeed by remarkable sites of play.

Conclusion: What will future parking lots look like?

With a car-less future on the horizon, it is timely to creatively re-think and reimagine the design, use and number of parking buildings and lots – from sites of low-cost accommodation to being redesigned for play and to facilitate urban sustainability, the parking lot of the future is far from a grey, bland, and uninspiring space. While not typically spaces designed with nudge theory, health or with 'the possibility of future renovation and renovation' (Xia et al., 2022, p. 2) in mind, this chapter has demonstrated the potential of thoughtfully designing parking lots. With conscious intention, one of the most mundane and overlooked elements of our built environment – the parking lot – might be positively transformed to become remarkable, and to nudge health, play, and sustainability, thus fostering human and planetary well-being.

Notes

1 To deep dive into parking lot design, Eran Ben-Joseph's engaging book, *Rethinking a lot*, is essential reading.
2 Watch a short video on the plans for Paris: https://www.weforum.org/agenda/2020/12/paris-parking-spaces-greenery-cities/.
3 If you are redesigning a parking lot, a valuable source of practical design tips is the US Environmental Protection Agency's Green Parking Lot Resource (2008).
4 View the roof and walking track here: https://www.greenroofs.com/projects/blue-cross-blue-shield-of-michigan-parking-garage/.
5 Watch this short film from Streetfilms on Amsterdam's plans: https://vimeo.com/339735964.
6 Online fitness Coach Meggin has designed a workout routine specifically for parking lots: https://youtu.be/8xElr8DrAqU.
7 Find out more and watch project videos here: https://beddown.org.au/what-we-do/.
8 Watch a video on the playable parking building rooftop here: https://jaja.archi/project/konditaget-luders/.

References

Ben-Joseph, E. (2012). *Rethinking a lot*. MIT Press.
Bertolini, L. (2020). From 'Streets for traffic' to 'Streets for people': Can street experiments transform urban mobility? *Transport Reviews*, *40*(6), 734–753.
C40. (2022). *About C40*. https://www.c40.org/about-c40
Cohen, D., Han, B., Derose, K., Williamson, S., Paley, A., & Batteate, C. (2016). CicLAvia: Evaluation of participation, physical activity and cost of an open streets event in Los Angeles. *Preventative Medicine*, *90*, 26–33. https://doi.org/10.1016/j.ypmed.2016.06.009
Fagnant, D. J., & Kockelman, K. (2015). Preparing a nation for autonomous vehicles: Opportunities, barriers and policy recommendations. *Transportation Research Part A: Policy and Practice*, *77*, 167–181.
Graça, M., Cruz, S., Monteiro, A., & Neset, T. (2022). Designing urban green spaces for climate adaptation: A critical review of research outputs. *Urban Climate*, *42*, 101126, https://doi.org/10.1016/j.uclim.2022.101126
Gysels, D. (2020). The Ghent living streets: Experiencing a sustainable and social future. In E. Curtis (Ed.), *The handbook of sustainable transport* (pp. 269–279). Edward Elgar.
Hamidi, A., Ramavandi, B., & Sorial, G. (2021). Sponge city — An emerging concept in sustainable water resource management: A scientometric analysis. *Resources, Environment and Sustainability*, *5*,100028. https://doi.org/10.1016/j.resenv.2021.100028
Harada, Y., & Whitlow, T. (2020). Urban rooftop agriculture: Challenges to science and practice. *Frontiers in Sustainable Food Systems*, *4*, https://doi.org/10.3389/fsufs.2020.00076
Holder, S. (2019). Finding home in a parking lot. *Bloomberg*. https://www.bloomberg.com/news/articles/2019-02-11/safe-parking-programs-help-homeless-sleeping-in-cars

Jensen, O., & Lanng, D. (2017). *Mobilities design: Urban designs for mobile situations*. Routledge.

Jordan, R. (2022). *Seven dead as 'Rain Bomb' unleashes intense flashfloods in Australia (online news)*. https://www.natureworldnews.com/articles/49635/20220228/seven-dead-rain-bomb-unleashes-intense-flashfloods-australia.htm

Kindermann, G., Domegan, C., Britton, E., Carlin, C., Isazad Mashinchi, M., & Ojo, A. (2021). Understanding the dynamics of green and blue spaces for health and wellbeing outcomes in Ireland: A systemic stakeholder perspective. *Sustainability, 13*, 9553. https://doi.org/10.3390/su13179553

Li, N., Jia, C., Fang, Z., Jiang, Z., Ahmed, A., Hao, D., Zhang, Z., & Luo, D. (2022). A u-shaped kinetic energy harvester for application in a near-zero energy parking system, *Sustainable Cities and Society, 81*, 103866. https://doi.org/10.1016/j.scs.2022.103866

Millard-Ball, A. (2021). Viewpoint: Turning streets into housing. *Journal of Transport and Land Use, 14*(1), 1061–1073. https://doi.org/10.5198/jtlu.2021.2020

Montero, S. (2017). Worlding Bogotá's Ciclovía: From urban experiment to international 'Best practice'. *Latin American Perspectives, 44*(2), 111–131. https://doi.org/10.1177/0094582X16668310

Nguyen, T. M. P., Davidson, K., & Coenen, L. (2020). Understanding how city networks are leveraging climate action: Experimentation through C40. *Urban Transform, 2*, 12. https://doi.org/10.1186/s42854-020-00017-7

Onishi, A., Cao, X., Ito, T., Shi, F., & Imura, H. (2010). Evaluating the potential for urban heat-island mitigation by greening parking lots. *Urban Forestry & Urban Greening, 9*, 323–332.

Pickerel, K. (2020). D.C.'s Metro Transit Authority to install 12.8 MW of solar canopies. *Solar Power World [online news]*. https://www.solarpowerworldonline.com/2020/07/d-c-s-metro-transit-authority-to-install-12-8-mw-of-solar-canopies/.

RethinkX. (2017). *Rethinking transportation 2020–2030: The disruption of transportation and the collapse of the internal-combustion vehicle and oil industries*. Retrieved from https://www.rethinkx.com/transportation#transportation-download

Roorda, C., Wittmayer, J., Henneman, P., Steenbergen, F., van Frantzeskaki, N., & Loorbach, D. (2014). *Transition management in the urban context: Guidance manual*. DRIFT, Erasmus University Rotterdam.

Ruddick, M. (2016). *Wild by design: Strategies for creating life-enhancing landscapes*. Island Press.

Rudge, K. (2021). The potential for community solar in Connecticut: A geospatial analysis of solar canopy siting on parking lots. *Solar Energy, 230*, 635–644. https://doi.org/10.1016/j.solener.2021.10.038

Sarmiento, O., Díaz del Castillo, A., Triana, C., Acevedo, M., Gonzalez, S., & Pratt, M. (2017). Reclaiming the streets for people: Insights from Ciclovías Recreativas in Latin America. *Preventative Medicine, 103*, S34–S40. https://doi.org/10.1016/j.ypmed.2016.07.028

Sustainable Technologies Evaluation Program. (2016). *Edwards Gardens parking lot retrofit: Case study*. https://sustainabletechnologies.ca/app/uploads/2016/08/Edwards-Gardens.pdf

Trautvetter, S. (2018). From asphalt to field – Parking lots as transitional urban landscapes. In *Conference proceedings of council of educators in landscape architecture (CELA)* (pp. 211–219). Virginia Tech.

Triana, C., Sarmiento, O., Bravo-Balado, A., González, S., Bolívar, M., Lemoine, P., Meisel, J., Grijalba, C., & Katzmarzyk, P. (2019). Active streets for children: The case of the Bogotá Ciclovía. *PLoS ONE*, *14*, e0207791. https://doi.org/10.1371/journal.pone.0207791

Walt Disney Company. (2020). *Disneyland Paris Embarks on one of the largest solar canopy energy projects in Europe* [Press release]. https://thewaltdisneycompany.com/disneyland-paris-embarks-on-one-of-the-largest-solar-canopy-energy-projects-in-europe/

Wehman-Brown, G. (2016). Home is where you park it: Place-making practices of car dwelling in the United States. *Space and Culture*, *19*(3), 251–259.

Xia, B., Fang, Y., Shen, H., Shen, J., & Pan, S. (2022). Sustainable renewal of underground parking space in the scenario of shared autonomous vehicles. *Buildings*, *12*(4). https://doi.org/10.3390/buildings12010004

10 Spending time and money

Redesigning shopping centres to be remarkable

The description below, written over a decade ago, presents suburban shopping centres in North America as dead and dying. In the aftermath of global lockdowns and social distancing measures during the COVID-19 pandemic, the viability of contemporary 'brick-and-mortar' retail is again in question. Already impacted by the rise of online shopping, the pandemics has further changed how consumers shop – and led some industry experts to use the term 'retail apocalypse' to describe the damage to the physical retail environment as increasing numbers of physical stores close their doors (Helm et al., 2020). In this chapter, therefore, we focus on how we might redesign the shopping centres experience to be more remarkable – nudging health, sustainability, and play.

> A mall is dead, its lifeblood of shoppers lured away by newer competition. The entrances are boarded up; the parking-lot asphalt is cracked and sprouting weeds; only memoires remain. What will happen next … malls are dying faster than they are getting built. It is very unlikely that the structure will ever serve as a conventional shopping mall again. Will it become a blight-spreading white elephant or a form-shifting phoenix rising from the ashes?
>
> (Williamson & Dunham-Jones, 2011, p. 204)

The origins of contemporary shopping centres: from community to consumerism

A shopping centre is a building that contains many separate shops but is managed as a single property. It enables users to easily do all their shopping at one central location, with the centre operators having one core purpose: to lease retail space for profit (Pitt & Musa, 2009). While the trade of goods and services is a key feature of human civilisation, originating with open air public markets where livestock, food, and other products (such as clothes and cooking utensils) could

DOI: 10.4324/9781003052746-12

be sold and purchased, shopping centres are a relatively recent addition to our consumer culture, originating in the United States in the 1920s (Feinberg & Meoli, 1991).

Austrian born architect Viktor Gruen pioneered the design of shopping malls in the United States and interestingly, his original vision for shopping centres was as a community centre where people would converge for shopping, cultural activity, and social interaction. Born Viktor Grünbaum, Viktor Gruen trained and practiced as an architect in Vienna and emigrated to the United States in 1938 to escape World War II where he changed his name to Gruen and formed the architectural firm, Gruen Associates. Gruen's firm designed the first regional shopping centre in 1954 (Northland Shopping Center in Detroit) and the first fully enclosed climate-controlled indoor shopping centre in 1956 (Southdale Centre, near Minneapolis), earning Gruen the moniker 'mall-maker'.

As people migrated to the suburbs, the need for auto-friendly suburban shopping centres grew. The standard street facing strip centre shopping offered essential goods and services, but limited space for safe social interactions (Scharoun, 2011). Gruen's vision for suburban shopping centres was much more than a simple 'collection of stores' (Wall, 2005, p. 57), but an enclosed city where consumers could safely stroll and interact – without dodging traffic.

Drawing on the landscape of European cities as inspiration, his utopian vision of shopping centres was to create an enjoyable and pedestrian friendly place for people to live, work, and shop,[1] recreating the diverse, lively, and walkable town centres and community spaces of his beloved Austria to provide 'isolated housewives and roaming teenagers places where they could meet and mingle' (Gruen, 2017, p. 17) in a 'market-town' or 'old town square' environment.

While Gruen's original vision for shopping centres has much in common with contemporary new urbanism design philosophies, which advocate for more walkable, denser, mixed-use communities, commercial realities meant his utopian vision of urbanism was not achieved in many of his designs. Developers, Gruen found, repeatedly 'hollowed out' his vision of shopping centres as mixed-use spaces that would connect to residential and commercial space, parks, medical care, childcare, libraries, and other public spaces. As Gruen (2017) explained in his 2017 book, *Shopping Town: Designing the city in Suburban America*, he designed the first fully enclosed indoor mall, Southdale Centre, around a lake and public park. However, focussed on reducing costs, developers ignored most of his plans, removing landscaping and sculpture to save money, and found that disorienting shoppers resulted in much higher revenue. And it is this enclosed shopping mall model has become the often formulaic standard for retail mall construction.

160   **Unremarkable spaces**

Gruen, who despised consumerism and later denounced shopping malls, became known for the design of stores and shopping centres as 'palaces of consumption' (Smiley, 2013, p. 6). The phrase 'the Gruen Effect'[2] is named after him and describes the moment when, after entering a shopping centre with one specific purpose in mind, a consumer – surrounded by an intentionally confusing layout and experience – is drawn in, loses track of their original intentions, and starts making impulse purchases. Who among us has not gone to the shopping centre with one specific purpose in mind and come home with piles of parcels – and not the one, intended purchase? That is the Gruen Effect. By suspending 'space, time, and weather' (Crawford, 1992, p. 16), contemporary shopping centres create a fantasy urbanism linking shopping with pleasure and diversion. Once a routine domestic task, shopping has become a pastime, a hobby (Miller, 2018), and entertainment, and is often even branded a patriotic duty, with the purposeful design of shopping centres encouraging consumption:

> All the familiar tricks of mall design – limited entrances, escalators placed only at the end of corridors, foundations and benches carefully positioned to entice shoppers into stores – control the flow of consumers through the numbingly repetitive corridors of all shops. The orderly processions of goods along endless aisles continuously stimulates the desire to buy.
>
> (Crawford, 1992, pp. 13–14)

Shopping centres as 'third spaces' – consumerism and/or community?

While shopping centres are of course, places of consumption and consumerism that seek retail dollars, they also provide a critical 'third space' – outside of home as first space, and work the second space. Urban sociologist Ray Oldenburg first introduced the concept of third spaces in his 1989 book '*The Great Good Place*', arguing that public social spaces bring us together in community and provide critical 'hangout' places, away from home and work. Third spaces can be cafes, pubs, malls, parks, churches, and libraries – or shopping centres. Oldenburg defines the characteristics of a third place as on neutral ground, with no obligation to stay or go; and levellers, meaning social status, do not matter in this space. The main activity is conversation; accessible and accommodating; regulars set the mood; not pretentious or ostentatious; playful in nature; and, critically, they provide a level of belonging that feels like a home away from home. As all-weather multi-purpose destinations, open to all members of a community, shopping centres have the potential to be a key third place – although, we acknowledge that this is a contested proposition with some arguing shopping centres are non-places, 'pseudo-public' spaces where architectural and other barriers (e.g. security guards) filter out 'undesirables'. Goss too reminds us:

> The shopping center appears to be everything that it is not. It contrives to be a public, civic place even though it is private and run for profit; it offers a place to commune and recreate, while it seeks retail dollars; and it borrows signs of other places and times to obscure its rootedness in contemporary capitalism.
>
> (Goss, 1993, p. 40)

'Retailtainment': from a place for shopping to a place for entertainment and experience?

With shopping now able to be done from home, online, and in pyjamas, there is increased attention on actively designing shopping centres to be exciting third places that, as well as offering a place for shopping, offer a place for unique experiences (see Pantano & Willems, 2021). Rigby (2011), for example, astutely notes, if traditional 'brick and mortar' retailers hope to successfully compete against their internet competitors, they must 'transform the big feature internet retailers lack – stores – from a liability into an asset. They must turn shopping into an entertaining, exciting, and emotionally engaging experience' (p. 65), as we see in Table 10.1.

Contemporary shopping centres are thus reimagining themselves, and the in-person shopping experience, in multiple ways. First, the design and function of shopping centres is evolving to be much more mixed-use, with apartment towers above the centre and shops co-located with childcare, libraries, gyms, and galleries. Second, to entice consumers to the centre and into stores, there is a significant

Table 10.1 Five critical changes in shopping centres for the post-pandemic world

1) Focus on safety and convenience, balancing consumers' desire for social interaction with their need for a safe, easy shopping experience.
2) Rethink the role of the store, emphasising the associate's role in facilitating an exceptional customer experience, and focusing on showroom, pop up locations and other innovation formats.
3) Make way for the food revolution, which will become the new anchor that brings visitors to the mall as less relevant fashion retailers move out.
4) Embrace technology, capitalising on digital tools to maximise productivity and efficiency and create experiences that are a dynamic and engaging.
5) Become a new destination, creating a multi-purpose environment that offers extensive leisure activities as well as other services, like office, residential, and cultural amenities.

Source: Deloitte (2021, p. 3).

focus on 'retailtainment', the combination of retail with entertainment, using 'ambience, emotion, sound and activity to get customers interested in the merchandise and in a mood to buy' (Ritzer, 1999). Table 10.1 illustrates how developers, landlords, and retailers must think very differently about the role, function, design, and operation of shopping centres to survive in our post-pandemic world:

> The mall of the future will be a destination that feeds the functional requirements of our lives as well as our need to be social. It will be a thriving community where people will live, work, play, and eat. It will not be your parents' mall—so much so that we might no longer call it a "mall" anymore at all.
>
> (Deloitte, 2021, p. 1)

In the remainder of this chapter, we imagine the future design of shopping centres.

Proposition 1: Nudging environmental sustainability through the design and operation of shopping centres

First, and perhaps paradoxically, we will start by exploring how the design and operations of shopping centres might be thoughtfully redesigned to nudge environmental sustainability. As we and others have discussed elsewhere (Cushing & Miller, 2020; Payne, 2021), while fast fashion and products dominate, those that are cheap and disposable, made and disposed of indiscriminately, there is a growing trend towards responsible product stewardship where those involved in designing, manufacturing, and selling products have a responsibility to ensure the environmental impacts of these products are minimised.

Creating a sustainable fashion retail experience: the case of ReTuna, Sweden

Shopping centres have a significant role to play in the sustainability agenda, in both their design and operations. While increasing numbers of us are committed to reducing our carbon footprint and living more sustainable lives (Miller, 2018), even the most sustainability-minded of us might not be aware that Sweden is home to the world's first ever second-hand shopping centre. A two-storey complex of second-hand stores located 70 miles west of Stockholm, everything in ReTuna[3] is recycled, re-used or sustainably produced. Opened in August 2015, ReTuna was initiated by the local municipality of Eskilstuna and is located five kilometres from the city, in an industrial area next to a waste recycling station.

ReTuna operates on a local circular fashion supply chain model. Local residents directly donate goods to the shopping centre, and goods are collected and distributed to tenants, whose rent covers these costs of both donated goods and the administrative costs associated with the reuse process of collection and sorting. The two storey 5,000 m^2 centre (3,600 leasable) is distributed over two floors, with fourteen stores/pop-up shops and a restaurant. Each day, approximately 750 people visit the shopping centre and 400 people dispose of goods at the waste recycling station (Hedegård et al., 2020).

Several factors make the ReTuna model unique. First, in traditional mall operations, management overseas general issues and the tenants manage the supply of products to their stores. At ReTuna, however, the supply of goods is via a reuse-based circular fashion supply chain comprised of three key processes: (1) collection of discarded products from consumers; (2) sorting, the inspection and categorisation of products according to quality and type; and (3) reprocessing – activities to enhance or restore functionality of the product, such as washing, repairing and redesigning (Payne, 2021). The local government operates ReTuna as a social enterprise, with the collection and sorting process, and many sales assistant roles, conducted by those in job training programmes. The only similarity to contemporary shopping centres is that retail sales remain the responsibility of tenants.

The factors that make ReTunda exciting and novel – the combination of a shopping centre with social enterprise and recycling/fashion reuse – also makes operations challenging. Achieving the full potential of this novel commercial fashion retail concept has been difficult, as few people have skills in fashion, reuse, and retail. Research has identified the issues facing ReTunda, namely only a small percentage of the donated clothes and textiles are sold, efficient sorting and reuse processes are lacking, the engaging visual merchandising typical of a fashion store is often missing, and there is no public transportation, limiting easy access for consumers (Hedegård et al., 2020). However, with estimates that the average garment today is worn only seven to ten times before being discarded (see Payne, 2021), there is no doubt we must think differently about shopping, fashion, and recycling. Initiatives such as ReTunda offer an exciting vision and roadmap for how conscious consumption and ethical fashion might become more mainstream, and also highlight an unusual and interesting retail option for other shopping centres to consider.

Making sustainable retail design mainstream: the world's most sustainable shopping centre, Burwood Brickworks

While a shopping centre like ReTuna, selling only recycled goods, remains an unconventional approach to sustainability, increasing numbers of centres are taking steps to address environmental sustainability – from reducing energy and water consumption to implementing sustainable

164 Unremarkable spaces

Figure 10.1 Adaptive re-use and sustainable retail at Burwood Brickworks.
Credit: Burwood Brickworks.

materials and environmentally friendly transport programmes. Sustainable retail design is becoming mainstream.

In Melbourne, Australia, Burwood Brickworks Shopping Centre has just been named the world's most sustainable shopping centre by the International Living Future Institute. As we detailed elsewhere (Cushing & Miller, 2020), the International Living Future Institute runs the Living Building Challenge® (LBC[4]), challenging the building sector to ask: *what if every single act of design and construction made the world a better place?* Using the analogy of a flower, because the ideal built environment should function as cleanly, efficiently and beautifully as a flower, and give more than it takes, the LBC has 20 imperatives, grouped into 7 'petals' (see Figure 10.1).

Burwood Brickworks Shopping Centre has achieved the first four LBC petals – Place, Health & Happiness, Materials, Beauty – and is working towards achieving Water, Energy and Equity by the end of 2022. Developed by Frasers Property Australia, this environmentally friendly urban regeneration project is the first LBC certified shopping centre in the world, and the first retail build in Australia to receive a 6 Green Star Design and As Built rating. About 20% of the site is dedicated to food growing purposes, featuring a 2,000 m^2 rooftop urban farm and restaurant, with 40% of the building's energy produced by 3,300 rooftop solar panels and a closed loop system treating all grey water on site for reuse. Biophilic design principles, which emphasise our connection to nature and living things (see Cushing & Miller,

2020), resulted in the urban farm, extensive use of skylights and solar tubes to provide natural light, with natural, recycled and repurposed materials and products used in the construction and fit out.

Designed by NH Architecture, with input from Russell & George, Burwood Brickworks Shopping Centre was purposely designed to 'reject big-box retail', with a mindset of adaptive reuse, sustainability and celebrating the unique sense of place critical in the design and build stage. The western façade, for example, incorporates recycled bricks made on the site more than half a century ago – a nod to the namesake of the project, Brickworks. Respecting and integrating local and indigenous cultural history was integral to the project. During the construction, local residents were asked to share three words about what their community meant to them; these words were painted on to salvaged bricks, and integrated into the Southern façade.

The site is on the traditional lands of the patrilineal Wurundjeri-wilam clan, with an expansive Aboriginal art installation in the unique style of Wurundjeri art, of symmetrical lines and diamond motifs, respecting and acknowledging this indigenous cultural history and connection to country. Figure 10.2 illustrates this striking indigenous mural, which is part of the internal ceiling of the centre and provides an important opportunity for local community members to engage with, be educated about and inspired by local indigenous art and culture. While the sustainability journey has at times been challenging and uncomfortable, the developers have also found it extremely rewarding:

> The vision for Burwood Brickworks was to redefine sustainability in retail by challenging ourselves in new and uncomfortable ways. It meant exposing ourselves to possible failure, inviting new levels of scrutiny, balancing commercial feasibility, challenging our project partners to take the journey with us, and investing time and resources into working with our tenants, so they could play their essential role.
>
> (Frasers Property, 2021)

Connecting with nature in shopping centres: 'de-malling' through biophilic design

While *Burwood Brickworks* is one of the first shopping centres in Australia to have an urban farm, globally, mall developers increasingly are integrating elements from nature – greenery, water, fountains, and animals – fish, birds, butterflies into their design – a strategy termed 'biophilic store design' (Joye et al., 2010).

Biophilia is the innate desire humans have to connect with nature and other living things, with a significant body of research showing

166 Unremarkable spaces

Figure 10.2 A striking indigenous mural on the internal ceiling of Burwood Brickwork.
Credit: Burwood Brickwork.

time spent in or around nature is calming and restorative (Kaplan, 1995). As the design of shopping centres evolves and changes, there is significant value in integrating elements of biophilic design – natural elements, features, and conditions of nature, the gardens, plants, nature, water, and animals – birds, butterflies, and fish, into its built retail form. As shopping centres across the globe add entertainment-oriented services and engage in a process of 'de-malling' (converting elements of enclosed malls into open-air shopping areas; Reynolds et al., 2002) to attract and retain customers, there is an opportunity for them to become more biophilic in their design.

By providing a 'dose of nature' while people shop, Rosenbaum et al. (2016; 2018) have convincingly argued that the thoughtful biophilic design of shopping malls could potentially enhance individual and societal well-being. In a series of experiments, Rosenbaum et al. (2018) varied whether college students viewed images of lifestyle (shopping) centres with or without greenery: they found a strong preference for the green biophilic designs. Such findings, combined with a consumer survey which suggested that green restoration encouraged loyalty and 'a shopper–mall bond' (Rosenbaum et al., 2016), led Rosenbaum and colleagues to encourage 'mall developers to empirically explore whether the greening of enclosed malls may offer these decaying retailing relics a new lifeline' (2016, p. 164).

Many shopping centres in Asia – where land is at premium – integrate biophilic features, rooftop gardens and farms. The developers of Hysan Place[5] in Hong Long, for example, explain they did not want to build another building 'that could be obsolete in 20-30 years time'. Driven by a desire to enliven the local community, they decided to build an urban farm on the rooftop of the shopping centre: every year 300 locals now farm the rooftop for three months – with the selection process managed through Hysan's in-house shopping loyalty programme.

Similarly, in Singapore, the seventh storey of the Funan shopping centre is an 18,000 square foot public Food Garden offering over 50 fruits and vegetables, including mushrooms, edible flowers, watermelon, and passion fruit. Operated by Edible Garden City[6] this urban farm offers volunteering opportunities and regular workshops, including adventure day camps for kids. As the images in Figure 10.3 illustrate, Funan Singapore has been recently redesigned by architecture and design firm Woods Bagot and won the 2021 Urban Land Institute's Asia Pacific Awards for Excellence, acknowledging the innovative mixed-use combination of retail, entertainment, leisure, dining, office, wellness, co-working, and co-living in the one urban location.

While an urban farm and centre redevelopment is a significant financial investment, smaller design decisions can also be impactful. Shopping centres and shops can implement visible design strategies fostering recycling. Clothing stores, for example, can offer clothing take-back schemes, collecting used clothing and textile waste, and make sustainable product choices in their store fit out. For example, when Danish fashion retailer Ganni[7] opened their first UK store in late 2019, the design choices expressed their commitment to being a closed-loop recycling company: the colourful marble display podiums,

Figure 10.3 The redesign of Funan Singapore, featuring an urban farm.
Credit: Architect & Interior Design: Woods Bagot. Director-in-Charge: Stephen Jones. Photographers: Darren Soh & Tim Franco.

bases and stool seats were made from scrap plastic leftovers, the wooden floors were recycled, and the rugs created from fabric from previous collections. Similarly, the interior of Aesop's store at Flinders Lane in Melbourne Australia features 3,000 recycled cardboard boxes, in counters and adjustable shelving walls. These boxes ship Aesop's products, so their purposeful use in their retail store is a public commitment to sustainable reuse.

How we design shopping centres matters. The decisions developers, designers, retailers, tenants, and consumers make has the potential to address multiple global sustainability challenges – of urbanisation, the

Table 10.2 A vision for the future – provocative scenarios for sustainable retail design

It's the year 2050 and all shopping centres are eco destinations. Sustainable materials are commonplace and obligatory as we live and co-exist in a circular economy. We cannot for one moment believe that at some point in our history, a time existed where there was no legal infrastructure in place so that brands could supply and produce products that were not environmentally friendly and that stores created an incredible volume of waste.

Back in 2030, we were grateful and relieved to see that the United Nations was able to achieve their environmental goals to have affordable and clean energy, fully sustainable consumption of natural resources and have climate change under control. Yet it was just 10 years before that, when the Australian bushfires shocked the world and a pandemic swept the globe, that humanity was forced to press pause on globalisation and international travel. It was an intensive and challenging time and people were not allowed to leave the house for prolonged periods. It was the year 2020 that the push for sustainability accelerated and mainstream consumption changed direction. Policymakers campaigned harder to pass laws to promote the emergence of the circular economy and companies worldwide adopted these constitutional acts. Consumers had decided there was no more planet B.

It currently is 2020. The future of our planet is uncertain. While COVID-19 and crisis management has been at the forefront of all business agendas, it is imperative companies do not lose sight of other emergencies such as the health of the environment. If we wish to safeguard our planet from the dangers of climate change, it is essential for retail design to develop a strategy to ensure the use of sustainable materials.

Source: Sheridan & Co (2020).

climate crisis, food security, and biodiversity. Whether it is the architectural design decisions to include solar energy, urban farms, and water-recycling, to connect people with nature or to integrate reuse and recycling processes, or smaller interior design decisions about material choices, our shopping centres can be much more sustainable and biophilic. By embracing circular economy principles in their planning, design and development, shopping centres and physical stores can signal to consumers the importance of conscious consumption – of reducing, reusing, upcycling, recycling, and re-thinking. And, of course, in our post-pandemic world, indoor air quality – and the purposeful integration of natural ventilation and outdoor spaces – will also be critical. As we reimagine the future of shopping centres to be more sustainable, the provocative futuristic scenarios in Table 10.2 provide some inspirational guidance.

Proposition 2: Nudging health by turning shopping centres into salutogenic places

As well as designing shopping centres to enhance planetary health, we argue that shopping centres can also be designed to be salutogenic, that is, health-promoting places. While this proposition too feels slightly paradoxical, in that shopping centres are privately owned with the aim of encouraging consumption, they are also important community sites that are safe, affordable, climate-controlled and, usually, relatively convenient to access. People of diverse ages and socio-cultural backgrounds use shopping centres in numerous different ways – for shopping yes, but also for socialising, for simply sitting and 'doing nothing', and, increasingly, for exercise.

'Mall-walking': providing places for people to exercise

Despite the well documented benefits of regular physical activity, most adults do not achieve the recommended guidelines of at least 150–300 minutes of moderate intensity aerobic physical activity throughout the week. In explaining why, as well as the barrier of busy lifestyles, many people note that the features of their local built environment – missing footpaths, poor lighting, traffic and crime, hilly terrain, inclement weather, and limited number of resting places – make neighbourhood walking challenging (see our chapter on redesigning streets for the importance of walkable neighbourhoods). With local streets sometimes deemed unsafe for exercise, growing numbers of people, and especially older people use the safe, accessible, and well-lit environment of their local shopping centre to engage in indoor 'mall-walking' (also termed '*mallercise*').

Most shopping centres offer a formal mall walking programme that is usually free or low-cost, with a small but growing body of research studies identifying the value especially in cities with cold climates and for older people, who find it safe, affordable, and convenient (Balsas, 2021; Farren et al., 2015; King et al., 2016). Importantly, a recent study noted that the leadership of the mall-walking group matters: effective *peer* walk leaders are most effective when they were optimistic, inclusive, and compassionate, as well as entertaining and adaptable (Kritz et al., 2020). For shopping centre operators wishing to establish a mall walking programme, Belza and colleagues (2015) have developed a free resource guide[8] which includes practical tips and strategies for starting and maintaining walking programmes, example posters and brochures, route maps and participation logs. Beyond mall walking groups however, shopping centres are beginning to offer other activities (e.g. tai chi, meditation yoga, pilates, exercise equipment/circuits/bootcamps, etc.) that (1) connect people while (2) facilitating physical and mental health.

To truly be salutogenic places, the future design and redesign of shopping centres should ideally integrate indoor and outdoor walking routes and exercise areas so as to provide another *healthy* reason for people to visit. In fact, Figure 10.4 illustrates how the redesign of the Funan Singapore shopping centre features an indoor climbing

Spending time and money 171

Figure 10.4 The redesign of Funan Singapore, featuring an indoor climbing wall and red biking track.

Credit: Architect & Interior Design: Woods Bagot. Director-in-Charge: Stephen Jones. Photographers: Darren Soh and Tim Franco.

wall and red biking track, which means users can easily run or cycle through this mall! With such innovative designs actively nudging healthy behaviours, the next evolution of shopping centres may well see the large concrete car parks that too often dominate shopping centres replaced by bicycle, e-bike or autonomous vehicle parking, as we discussed in the previous chapter.

Proposition 3: That the design of shopping centres can nudge play

Here we turn to the proposition that purposeful engagement with playable design principles might help rejuvenate shopping centres to create a 'playspace' that reflects the ludic (playful) and hedonic (pleasurable) character of a retail environment. Many consumers desire this novelty and fantasy, and there are numerous examples across the globe of shopping centres that have made play central to their brand. The humorous quote below, now over thirty years old, is a powerful reminder that some consumers visit shopping centres purely for the entertainment:

> In truth, I don't go to the malls to shop. Sure I might buy something, but it's not opportunity or need that brings me to a mall - it's the glitter and glitz, the chance to mingle … A good mall is like a good man: it offers entertainment, excitement and enlightenment.
> (Gershman, 1988, p. 43)

In thinking about playable design in shopping centres, we start with the most common example: entertaining kids and families, through playgrounds. While many centres still only offer basic play equipment, a thoughtfully designed playground can drive visitation duration and frequency, while simultaneously and positively differentiating the centre as a place for family. Play structures inside malls come in many different forms, usually with strategically placed food and family stores nearby, encouraging families to spend more time and money in the centre. Playground equipment manufacturers Proludic[9] advise that designers of play areas in shopping centres should consider: *the number of children and their age groups; offering a diverse range of engaging play activities; a layout that accommodates both children and parents; blending in with the architectural identity and brand of the centre, as well as local features and identity; and creating surprise and interest, through a striking signature feature.*

While play equipment entertains younger children, whether shopping centres are or should be places of play for tweens and teens is debatable. However, the design of American skate/leisure shoe brand House of Vans' London store exemplifies the type of experience and

Spending time and money   173

playable design principles needed to draw people away from online shopping and back into physical shops. Located beneath the Waterloo rail tracks, House of Vans' London store is a mixed-use creative venue comprising a three-tier indoor concrete skate park, cinema and art gallery displaying vintage Vans memorabilia, live music space for 850 people, as well as a café, numerous bars, 'Vans labs' creative spaces and a retail store. A cultural hub for skateboarding, Vans London is an extreme example of 'retailtainment' in action.

As shopping centres evolve into multi-functional retail-leisure complexes (Pantano & Willems, 2021), engaging with playable design perspectives provides the fresh 'out-of-the-box' thinking needed for true innovation and evolution. Along with issues of retail mix, locality and accessibility, the ambience and atmospherics of a shopping centre – design details of colour, lighting, floor, seating, skylights, and entertainment programming including activities, music and the like, help influence visitation patterns. Making a centre more 'playable', could therefore help attract consumers, creating a unique competitive advantage.

What 'playable design' looks like will be different for each centre, depending on the local culture and context. Across the globe, there are existing large-scale examples: the Dubai mall is home to the largest indoor aquarium in the world; the Berjaya Times Square in Kuala Lumpur hosts Asia's largest indoor theme park; and, the West Edmonton Mall in Canada hosts a water park, ice palace, adventure golf and hotels. Increasingly, shopping centre owners, designers and retailers work to create that 'wow' factor experience or installation that attracts consumers for a fun, memorable and Instagram moment. While few shopping centres will have the means and desire to build large aquariums or an indoor concrete skate park, all can engage with playful design ideas to help develop a unique local destination that introduces a sense of fun, delight, and creative play into daily life.

Conclusion

In closing, this chapter has highlighted how shopping centres can be transformed from bland and unremarkable 'big boxes' to important third places and sites of community connection that nudge health, sustainability and play through their thoughtful design. To survive the 'retail apocalypse' of our post-pandemic world, shopping centres must actively reinvent themselves as mixed-use spaces that combine retail, residential, office, entertainment, health and wellness, leisure, childcare, aged care, community activities, and civic services, such as libraries and government services. This mixed used design approach needs to be alongside other engaging and novel experiences that engage

174 Unremarkable spaces

consumers, while nudging sustainability, health, and play. Embarking on this change process is essential, because if 'malls don't reinvent themselves, there will be no mall of the future' (Deloitte, 2021, p. 14).

Notes

1 Commissioned by Victor Gruen Associates, this rare 20-minute 1968 documentary film outlines Fresno's urban renewal campaign of the 1960s which led to the construction of the Fulton Mall as a national model for solving the urban crisis of the post-war era. It begins with a compelling quote from Lyndon B Johnson - our society will never be great until our cities are great: https://www.youtube.com/watch?v=bdTS_LLJvcw.
2 Listen to an engaging podcast about architect Viktor Gruen and The Gruen Effect here: https://99percentinvisible.org/episode/the-gruen-effect/.
3 Watch a video on ReTuna here: https://www.youtube.com/watch?v=K3_qdo2NWjM.
4 See https://living-future.org/lbc-3_1/basics/
5 Watch here: https://www.youtube.com/watch?v=aHf2wgr5rP8
6 Watch here: https://www.ediblegardencity.com/
7 See https://www.ganni.com/en-au/responsibility-planet.html
8 See https://www.cdc.gov/physicalactivity/downloads/mallwalking-guide.pdf
9 See https://www.proludic.com.au/who-are-you/shopping-centres/

References

Balsas, C. (2021). The reinvention of indoor walking for sustainable non-motorized active living in winter cities. *Journal of Human Behavior in the Social Environment*, *31*(5), 626–641.

Belza, B., Allen, P., Brown, D., Farren, L., Janicek, S., Jones, D., King, D., Marquez, D., Miyawaki, C., & Rosenberg, D. (2015). *Mall walking: A program resource guide*. University of Washington Health Promotion Research Center.

Crawford, M. (1992). The world in a shopping mall. In M. Sorkin (Ed.), *Variations on a theme park: The new American city and the end of public space* (pp. 3–30). Hill and Wang.

Cushing, D., & Miller, E. (2020). *Creating great places: Evidence-based urban design for health and wellbeing*. Routledge.

Deloitte. (2021). The future of the mall: Building a new kind of destination for the post-pandemic world. *Deloitte Canada*. Retrieved from https://www2.deloitte.com/content/dam/Deloitte/ca/Documents/consumer-industrial-products/ca-future-of-the-mall-en-AODA.pdf

Farren, L., Belza, B., Allen, P., Brolliar, S., Brown, D., Cormier, M., & Rosenberg, D. (2015). Mall walking program environments, features, and participants: A scoping review. *Preventing Chronic Disease*, *12*, E129. https://doi.org/10.5888/pcd12.150027

Feinberg, R., & Meoli, J. (1991). A brief history of the mall. *Advances in Consumer Research*, *18*(1), 426–471.

Frasers Property. (2021). *Burwood Brickworks recognised as the world's most sustainable shopping centre* [press release]. https://www.burwoodbrickworks.shopping/News/2021/04/24/Living-Building-Challenge-Petal-Certification

Gershman, S. (1988). Mad about the mall. *Travel & Leisure*, 43–48.

Goss, J. (1993). The 'Magic of the mall': An analysis of form, function, and meaning in the contemporary retail built environment. *Annals of the Association of American Geographers, 83*(1), 18–47.

Gruen, V. (2017). *Shopping town: Designing the city in suburban America.* University of Minnesota Press.

Hedegård, L., Gustafsson, E., & Paras, M. (2020). Management of sustainable fashion retail based on reuse: A struggle with multiple logics. *The International Journal of Retail, Distribution and Consumer Research, 30*(3), 311–330.

Helm, S., Kim, S., & van Riper, S. (2020). Navigating the 'retail apocalypse': A framework of consumer evaluations of the new retail landscape. *Journal of Retailing and Consumer Services, 54*, 101683. https://doi.org/10.1016/j.jretconser.2018.09.015

Joye, J., Willems, K., Brengman, M., & Wolf, K. (2010). The effects of urban greenery on consumer experience: Reviewing the evidence from a restorative perspective. *Urban Forestry & Urban Greening, 9*(1), 57–64.

Kaplan, S. (1995). The restorative benefits of nature: Toward an integrative framework. *Journal of Environmental Psychology, 15*(3), 169–182.

King, D. K., Allen, P., Jones, D. L., Marquez, D. X., Brown, D. R., Rosenberg, D., Janicek, S., Allen, L., & Belza, B. (2016). Safe, affordable, convenient: Environmental features of malls and other public spaces used by older adults for walking. *Journal of Physical Activity & Health, 13*(3), 289–295.

Kritz, M., Thøgersen-Ntoumani, C., Mullan, B., McVeigh, J., & Ntoumanis, N. (2020). Effective peer leader attributes for the promotion of walking in older adults. *The Gerontologist, 60*(6), 1137–1148.

Miller, E. (2018). 'My hobby is global warming and peak oil': Sustainability as serious leisure. *World Leisure Journal, 60*(3), 209–220.

Oldenburg, R. (1989). *The good great place: Cafes, coffee shops, community centers, general stores, bars, and how they get you through the day.* Paragon Books.

Pantano, E., & Ws, K. (2021). *Retail in a new world: Recovering from the pandemic that changed the world.* Emerald.

Payne, A. (2021). *Designing fashion's future: Present practice and tactics for sustainable change.* Bloomsbury.

Pitt, M., & Musa, Z. (2009). Towards defining shopping centres and their management systems. *Journal of Retail & Leisure Property, 8*, 39–55.

Reynolds, K., Ganesh, J., & Luckett, M. (2002). Traditional malls vs factory outlets: Comparing shopper typologies and implications for retail strategy. *Journal of Business Research, 5*(9), 687–696.

Rigby, D. (2011). The future of shopping. *Harvard Business Review, 89*, 65–76.

Ritzer, G. (1999). *Enchanting a disenchanted world: Revolutionizing the means of consumption.* Sage.

Rosenbaum, M., Losada, M., & Contreras, G. (2016). The restorative potential of shopping malls. *Journal of Retailing and Consumer Services, 31*, 157–165.

Rosenbaum, M., Ramirez, G., & Camino, J. (2018). A dose of nature and shopping: The restorative potential of biophilic lifestyle center designs. *Journal of Retailing and Consumer Services, 40*, 66–73.

Scharoun, L. (2011). Utopia lost? The significance of the shopping mall in American culture and the effects of its decline on the American public. *The Australasian Journal of Popular Culture, 1*(2), 227–245.

Sheridan & Co. (2020). Why retail design needs to incorporate sustainable materials and embrace reuse as a design tool. *Blog post.* Retrieved

11 March 2022 from https://www.sheridanandco.com/news/why-retail-design-needs-to-incorporate-sustainable-materials-and-embrace-reuse-as-a-design-tool/

Smiley, D. (2013). *Pedestrian modern: Shopping and American architecture, 1925–1956*. University of Minnesota Press.

Wall, A. (2005). *Victor Gruen: From urban shop to new city*. Actar.

Williamson, J., & Dunham-Jones, E. (2011). *Retrofitting suburbia: Urban design solutions for redesigning suburbs*. Wiley.

Conclusion

Redesigning the unremarkable – thinking differently

From rubbish bins and benches, to parking lots and shopping centres, this book has traversed a wide range of unremarkable elements and spaces of our built environment driven by one simple overarching objective: to help us think differently and more innovatively about them and how they are designed. Looking around us at the environments we use every day, we must question whether the elements and spaces can be redesigned in ways that better serve our needs and the needs of the planet. We need to ask, how can these elements and spaces be more sustainable, salutogenic and playable? How can they be more remarkable?

As our thinking always starts with our current frames of thought, envisioning a different future is not easy. *Redesigning the Unremarkable* guides us to think beyond current constraints, to creatively imagine, what might be. What might a rubbish bin look like if it was designed with the lens of sustainability or salutogensis? How might a multi-use trail or shopping centre be more sustainable? Could traditionally 'left-over spaces' such as underpasses, parking lots and stairwells, be transformed into places that foster social connections, play, and physical activity – that is, become playable and salutogenic spaces?

Redesigning the Unremarkable has been written to start a new conversation, where citizens, policymakers, creatives, and professional architects and designers collaborate to *think differently* about what is possible as we design and redesign our built environment. As we consider global challenges that include climate change and COVID-19, we must focus on the role of micro-environments. We must re-consider daily life and engage in positive 'what-if' future-oriented conversations to learn how we can do better.

We hope this book will inspire and inform. There is a lot of work to be done, but we are excited about the possibilities of redesigning the mundane and forgotten elements and spaces around us. There are already a lot of great ideas that we can learn from and build on, and we hope that by sharing some of these it can foster excitement about the alternative sustainable, playable, and salutogenic visions for our future.

DOI: 10.4324/9781003052746-13

Appendix

The following activities can be used to better understand theory storming and nudge theory and incorporate these concepts into your practice. They can be used to evaluate existing spaces, or to conceptualise new designs. These can be used with students or during workshops with community members.

Activity 1: Theory-storming activity

Once you have assessed a site or location and understand the challenges, opportunities, and constraints, use the theories listed below (plus any others you think are relevant), to evaluate potential design options. You can refer to *Creating Great Places* (Cushing & Miller, 2020) for more information about each theory. You can also use the table during the design process to understand the challenges with an existing space.

1) Affordance Theory.
2) Prospect-Refuge Theory.
3) Personal Space Theory.
4) Sense of Place Theory.
5) Place Attachment Theory.
6) Biophilic Design Theory.

Use the table to write up the potential design interventions that represent or address the theories. An example has been provided. Add rows to the table as needed. Our theory-storming activity builds on Edward de Bono's thinking hats concept, in that you could ask participants to explicitly 'put on the hat of biophilic design theory'–and advocate for that lens in their group.

Relevant Theory	Proposed Design Solution that Addresses the Theory
Example: Prospect-Refuge Theory (see without being seen)	Example: Arrange benches on the outer edge of the stage area and provide vegetation and a mid-height wall behind the benches to provide protection and a sense of security. Benches will have a good view of the activities within the space and will be arranged for viewing.

Activity 2: The nudge challenge

This activity is designed to be completed in small groups. However, if that is not possible, it can be done by an individual. In small groups (if possible), brainstorm at least six design nudges that could be implemented in (choose a site or location). The nudges provide options for people using the space and encourage them to make a decision that is beneficial for their health and wellbeing or the health of the planet. As an exercise, try to come up with the following:

- Two nudges that encourage sustainability
- Two nudges that encourage playability
- Two nudges that encourage health and wellbeing (salutogenic environments)

To help you brainstorm your nudges, use the EAST Framework (Service et al., n.d.):

- Make it Easy
- Make it Attractive
- Make it Social
- Make it Timely

Tasks: (adapted from The Behavioural Insights Team 'EAST Four simple ways to apply behavioural insights'):

1) **Define the outcome**
   Identify exactly what behaviour is to be influenced, based on the general goals above. What choice do you want people to make? Why?
2) **Understand the context**
   Discuss the situations and groups involved in the activity or behaviour and understand the context from their perspective. Use this opportunity to develop new insights and design a sensitive and feasible design intervention.
3) **Draw or plan out your intervention**
   This is likely to be an iterative process that returns to the two steps above. Use your design skills to come up with something that will nudge your chosen behaviour. Use the examples throughout the book to be inspired.
4) **Test, learn, and adapt (iterate)**
   Draw or build a sketch model of your nudges to 'test' them with other groups/people. Getting feedback and testing out ideas is part of the design process and will provide additional ideas and understandings.

Rating the Nudges:

After you have developed a series of nudges, evaluate them based on their perceived effectiveness. You can also create a survey to give to others in order to have them rate the nudges and how likely they would be to work.

1 = Likely to be very effective
2 = Likely to be moderately effective
3 = Not likely to be effective

References

Cushing, D., & Miller, E. (2020). *Creating great places: Evidence-based urban design for health and wellbeing*. Routledge.

Service, O., Hallsworth, M., Halpern, D., Algate, F., Gallagher, R., Nguyen, S., Ruda, S., Sanders, M., Pelenur, M., Gyani, A., Harper, H., Reinhard, J., & Kirkman, E. E. (n.d.). EAST: Four simple ways to apply behavioural insights. Cabinet Office & Nesta, Downloaded 9 October 2022 from https://www.bi.team/wp-content/uploads/2015/07/BIT-Publication-EAST_FA_WEB.pdf

Acknowledgements

The contract for this book was secured in late 2019, just before the COVID-19 pandemic – which has, of course, disrupted and changed our lives. As we re-evaluate our practices, routines, and the use and design of everyday urban environments, our hope is that this book might spark some unconventional thinking and the creation of remarkable spaces. We would like to particularly acknowledge and thank our family, friends, and colleagues for their support, patience, and understanding as we wrote this book. We also thank our writing coach and editor, Karyn Gonano, for her feedback and support. Finally, and most importantly, we especially acknowledge and thank the design practices, researchers, and community members from across the globe for their engagement in sharing with us examples of remarkable (and unremarkable) elements and spaces, and allowing us to use some of their images – we appreciate your generosity.

Index

ageing 48
art 9–10, 18–19, 34, 38, 40–44, 54–56, 71–74, 104–111, 116–124, 127–135

bikeways 22, 126, 128–133, 135, 137–138
bins 8, 13, 20–21, 29–41, 48, 79, 129, 177
Brisbane 1, 2, 10, 15, 19, 51, 101, 112, 130, 131, 135, 145
boring 2, 90, 109
broken window theory 4, 5, 6, 9, 10, 12, 86, 87, 98, 130
buildings 13, 17. 23, 40, 62–64, 66–68, 72–76, 81–84, 88–89, 92, 112, 116, 141, 164

Canada 47, 53, 79, 100, 104, 132, 145
change 2–3, 7–10, 12–13, 21–22, 25, 29, 32–34, 38, 41, 46, 72, 101, 104, 112, 138, 177, 179
child 12, 37, 127
COVID 15, 46, 52, 112–113, 116, 124, 150, 158, 169, 177, 181
crime 4, 6, 25, 53, 60,63, 97, 119, 129, 132, 170; CPTED 6, 63
cues to care 4, 6, 9, 12, 79, 88, 101

data 17, 19, 22, 79, 123, 128, 144
design 12–15, 17–19; design competitions 8, 35, 56

fun 6–9, 17–18, 22, 33, 36–39, 55–56, 81–88, 90–92
future 18, 24–26, 40, 122, 141, 155, 162–164

guidelines 170; Koala sensitive 86; physical activity 65, 77; street design 115, 118

indigenous design 21, 87, 100, 109, 129, 165–166
interaction 1, 6, 9, 17, 32, 36–39, 50–52, 61, 66, 85, 120, 131, 154

learning 93, 120

Melbourne 10, 116, 117, 150, 164

Netherlands 75, 107, 108, 135, 136, 149
New York 1, 10, 35, 40, 45, 55, 63, 72, 100, 105, 112, 115, 129, 132
nudge 4, 6, 7–9, 12–13, 15, 25–26, 33–34, 37, 41, 72–76, 119–122

park 9, 11, 15, 17, 21, 30, 39, 40, 44, 45, 46, 52, 54, 55, 56, 78, 88, 89, 90, 100, 101, 104, 105, 106, 119, 120, 127, 128, 159, 160, 173; parklet 116, 120, 121, 122; skate park 100, 105, 106, 173
parking lots 2, 21–22, 122, 141–156, 177
physical activity 8, 10, 19, 46, 47, 62, 63, 65, 66, 72, 75, 79, 104, 114, 118, 120, 126–128, 135, 138, 148, 149, 170, 177
poems 29, 41, 43, 78

risk 46, 85, 123, 140

Index 183

safe 7, 10, 26, 46, 52, 61–66, 67, 74, 79–80, 83, 87, 100–101, 104, 159–161, 169–170, 175
seats 17, 45, 47–48, 51–52, 60, 168
shopping centres 21–22, 30, 112, 158–175
Singapore 73, 88, 89, 123, 167, 168, 170, 171
social 9, 11, 13–17, 24, 42–47, 50–52, 63, 66, 75–76, 79, 98, 105, 114–116, 124, 128
stairs 7–8, 12–15, 24, 62–69, 72–77, 121, 153–154
sustainability 34, 39, 40–43, 56, 72, 76–77, 156, 62–163, 169

sustainable 3, 7, 9, 12–15, 31–33, 42–43, 56
Sydney 65, 68, 123

technology 36–38

underpasses 22, 88, 97–110, 177

virtual 36, 80

walk 19, 24, 37, 44, 47, 105, 108, 115, 118, 125–131, 135
walls 13, 20–21, 44, 78–93, 103, 109, 120, 143, 146, 168
William H. Whyte 44, 45, 52

Yarn-bombing 2, 3, 9, 10, 15, 88–91

Milton Keynes UK
Ingram Content Group UK Ltd.
UKHW022038270923
429517UK00006B/26